DILBERT®
Gives You the Business

A DILBERT® BOOK

BY **SCOTT ADAMS**

Andrews McMeel
Publishing

Kansas City

For Pam, The Queen of Lists

Other DILBERT books from Andrews McMeel Publishing

Don't Step in the Leadership
Journey to Cubeville
I'm Not Anti-Business, I'm Anti-Idiot
Seven Years of Highly Defective People
Casual Day Has Gone Too Far
Fugitive from the Cubicle Police
Still Pumped from Using the Mouse
It's Obvious You Won't Survive by Your Wits Alone
Bring Me the Head of Willy the Mailboy!
Shave the Whales
Dogbert's Clues for the Clueless
Build a Better Life by Stealing Office Supplies
Always Postpone Meetings with Time-Wasting Morons

For ordering information, call 1-800-642-6480.

DILBERT® is a registered trademark of United Feature Syndicate, Inc.

DOGBERT and DILBERT appear in the comic strip DILBERT®, distributed by United Feature Syndicate, Inc.

www.dilbert.com

www.andrewsmcmeel.com

04 05 06 07 08 09 10 BAM 15 14 13 12 11 10 9 8 7 6 5

ISBN: 0-7407-0003-0 (paperback)
        0-7407-0338-2 (hardcover)

Library of Congress Catalog Card Number: 99-61204

━━━━━━ ATTENTION: SCHOOLS AND BUSINESSES ━━━━━━

Andrews McMeel books are available at quantity discounts with bulk purchase for educational, business, or sales promotional use. For information, please write to: Special Sales Department, Andrews McMeel Publishing, 4520 Main Street, Kansas City, Missouri 64111.

If you're a typical *Dilbert* reader, the question in your mind right now is, "How can I use this book as a weapon to embarrass my enemies?"

I realize that's a gross generalization. The more noble-minded *Dilbert* readers are thinking, "How can I use this book as a weapon to embarrass my friends?" Still others are wondering how they can steal this book from their friends and call it "borrowing."

But whether you have friends or not, I'm here to help.

Responding to an avalanche of suggestions, I have gathered all the most-requested *Dilbert* strips about the business world and organized them by topic. If you want to find all the best *Dilbert* comics on, for example, budgeting, or programming, or performance reviews, or engineering, or marketing, they're here, along with dozens of other topics.

This is a huge improvement over the old method where you might have access to only one or two *Dilbert* comics to make your point. It's nearly impossible to do a thorough job of mocking someone when you are so limited in your choice of comics. Thanks to this book, that will never be a problem again. Now you can show someone a few dozen *Dilbert* strips on the same topic and be certain your message gets across. You'll never again have to deal with the same annoying question, "Are you trying to tell me something?"

It wasn't easy to pull this book together. I stayed up all night, with comics spread around on my furniture and the floor, sorting them into categories. My cat, Sarah, helped by rolling around in the piles until the static electricity made the strips stick to her fur. It wasn't much help, but I don't pay her much either. If you find any duplicates or strips out of place, blame my cat. If the whole book is missing, your friends probably "borrowed" it.

Speaking of friends, you might want to join Dogbert's New Ruling Class and rule by his side when he conquers the planet and makes everyone else our domestic servants. Joining is as easy as signing up for the free *Dilbert* newsletter, published about four times a year whenever I feel like it.

To subscribe, send a blank E-mail to dilbert-text-on@list.unitedmedia.com.
To unsubscribe, send a blank E-mail to dilbert-off@list.unitedmedia.com.
If you have problems with the automated subscription write to newsletter@unitedmedia.com.

You can also subscribe via snail mail:
     Dilbert Mailing List
     United Media
     200 Madison Ave.
     New York, NY 10016

S. Adams

Scott Adams

Jobs

Job Impediments

LET'S START BY INTRODUCING OURSELVES.

I'M SUSAN BLOCK FROM I.T.G. I WORK FOR EMILY WOOTEN.

I'M MAX BLUMF. I WORK FOR SUSAN.

I'M ALICE. I WORK FOR... UH... I ...

AAAGH!!! I'M FILLED WITH SHAME BY ASSOCIATION!!!

WHY ME? WHY WHY WHY

PLEASE TAKE ME TO YOUR GROUP! I'M NOT TAINTED!!!

CAN WE START OVER? I FORGOT WHO THE FIRST THREE PEOPLE ARE.
SOB

IT HAS COME TO MY ATTENTION THAT YOU USED THE FAX FOR PERSONAL BUSINESS.

I SENT THE FAX DURING LUNCH. IT WAS A LOCAL CALL.

YOU'RE USING UP ALL OF OUR FAX PAPER.

NO, I SENT A FAX. THE PAPER DOESN'T TRAVEL THROUGH THE PHONE LINES.
REALLY?

YOU USED THE COMPANY'S ELECTRICITY.

I HAD A FRIEND FAX US A WAD OF EXTRA ELECTRICITY.

I'M USING IT RIGHT NOW TO POWER MY PC.

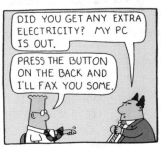
DID YOU GET ANY EXTRA ELECTRICITY? MY PC IS OUT.
PRESS THE BUTTON ON THE BACK AND I'LL FAX YOU SOME.

YOUR PROPOSAL DOESN'T ADDRESS THE ALTERNATIVES.

THERE AREN'T ANY REASONABLE ALTERNATIVES.

THERE ARE ALWAYS ALTERNATIVES! GIVE ME ALTERNATIVES!!

NO WONDER NOTHING GETS DONE AROUND HERE — NOT ENOUGH ALTERNATIVES.

"WE COULD LOBBY THE GOVERNMENT TO GIVE TAX BREAKS TO ALL IDIOT-RUN BUSINESSES."

"I COULD QUIT THIS STUPID JOB AND START A NEW CAREER HANDING OUT TOWELS AT THE GYM."

"OR WE COULD USE COW CHIPS INSTEAD OF MICROCHIPS AND SAVE MILLIONS."

WHAT'S A COW CHIP?
THIS JOB WOULD BE AN EXAMPLE.

THE WORST HE CAN DO IS FIRE ME...

BOSS, I NEED TO TALK TO YOU.

I FEEL YOU DON'T RESPECT ME...

IT'S AN INTANGIBLE THING...
SNEEZE COMING...

I SEE IT IN YOUR BODY LANGUAGE...
AAH...

...AND SOMETIMES THE THINGS YOU SAY...
RRRRIIP

CHOOO

THIS HAS BEEN SOMETHING LESS THAN A VICTORY FOR WORKERS EVERYWHERE.

MY NEW STYLE OF MANAGEMENT IS EXHAUSTING ME.

I HEARD SOME PEOPLE TALKING ABOUT "MBWA" OR "MANAGEMENT BY WALKING AROUND."

I WALKED ALL THE WAY TO THE PARK AND BACK. BUT I CAN'T SAY THAT I SEE MUCH IMPROVEMENT AROUND HERE.

I'VE BEEN SAYING FOR YEARS THAT "EMPLOYEES ARE OUR MOST VALUABLE ASSET."

IT TURNS OUT THAT I WAS WRONG. MONEY IS OUR MOST VALUABLE ASSET. EMPLOYEES ARE NINTH.

I'M AFRAID TO ASK WHAT CAME IN EIGHTH.

CARBON PAPER.

I'M STARTING AN INTERDISCIPLINARY TASK FORCE TO STUDY OUR DECISION-MAKING PROCESS.

SO, YOU'RE USING A BAD DECISION-MAKING PROCESS TO DECIDE HOW TO FIX OUR BAD DECISION-MAKING PROCESS?

I DON'T KNOW HOW ELSE WE COULD FIND THE SOURCE OF OUR PROBLEM.

X-RAY YOUR SKULL?

I'M RUNNING LATE. BUT SINCE I'M A VICE PRESIDENT YOU'LL HAVE TO WAIT IN THE HALLWAY.

YOU'LL BE ABLE TO JUDGE YOUR RELATIVE WORTH BY OBSERVING WHAT THINGS I DO WHILE YOU WAIT.

HE'S TEACHING HIMSELF THE BANJO.

BOSS TYPES

FIND YOUR BOSS ON THIS HANDY REFERENCE.

HOSTAGE TAKER: TRAPS YOU IN YOUR CUBICLE AND TALKS YOUR EARS OFF.

BLAH BLAH

OW!!

FRAUD: USES VIGOROUS HEAD-NODDING TO SIMULATE COMPREHENSION.

THEN WE'LL SUBNET OUR I.P. ADDRESSES.

OH YEAH OH YEAH

MOTIVATIONAL LIAR: HAS NO CLUE WHAT YOU DO BUT SAYS YOU'RE THE BEST.

NOBODY CAN DO WHAT YOU DO!!

EXCEPT A MUSHROOM.

OVER PROMOTED: TRIES TO MASK INCOMPETENCE WITH POOR COMMUNICATION.

LET'S QUALITIZE OUR PARADIGM SO WE DON'T OVER INUNDATE WITH DATUMS.

WEASEL: TAKES CREDIT FOR YOUR HARD WORK.

THIS BONUS IS FOR BRILLIANTLY FORCING YOUR STAFF TO WORK 80 HOUR WEEKS.

IT WASN'T EASY!

MOSES: PERPETUALLY WAITS FOR CLEAR SIGNALS FROM ABOVE.

DON'T DO ANYTHING IMPORTANT YET.

NEVER HAVE.

PERFECT BOSS: DIES OF NATURAL CAUSES ON A THURSDAY AFTERNOON.

SHOULD WE DO SOMETHING?

THREE DAY WEEKEND!

YOU ALL KNOW OUR PRESIDENT, MISTER GOODENRICH. HE'S HERE TO ANSWER ANY QUESTIONS YOU HAVE.

WHY AREN'T THERE ANY WOMEN OR MINORITIES IN SENIOR MANAGEMENT POSITIONS?

WE THINK WOMEN ARE FOR MAKING BABIES. AS FOR MINORITIES, WE FEAR THEM.

HOW CAN YOU JUSTIFY YOUR TEN MILLION DOLLAR SALARY WHEN PROFITS ARE DOWN?

HA HA! THE BOARD OF DIRECTORS ARE FRIENDS OF MINE AND IT'S NOT THEIR MONEY THEY'RE SPENDING.

WHY DOES THE COMPANY KEEP TALKING ABOUT EMPLOYEE TRAINING WHILE AT THE SAME TIME SLASHING THE TRAINING BUDGET?

WE THINK YOU'RE TOO DUMB TO TRAIN. WE'LL HIRE PEOPLE FROM THE OUTSIDE IF WE NEED TALENT.

I MUST SAY, YOUR HONESTY IS KIND OF REFRESHING.

AND YOU'RE ALL FIRED FOR ASKING QUESTIONS.

DOES YOUR BOSS GIVE YOU ORDERS AND LATER DENY IT? DO YOU GET IN TROUBLE FOR DOING WHAT YOU'RE TOLD?

YES

THE "DOGBERT DETECTIVE AGENCY" WILL VIDEOTAPE IT ALL AND EMBARRASS YOUR BOSS WITH PROOF!

WHAT??! WHY DID YOU DO THIS??!

THIS IS THE HAPPIEST MOMENT OF MY CAREER.

LIGHTS!

DILBERT, I'D LIKE YOU TO MEET BEN, OUR NEWEST FAST-TRACK MANAGER.

HI

BEN HAS NO REAL EXPERIENCE BUT HE'S VERY TALL, SO WE KNOW HE'LL GO FAR.

I ALSO HAVE EXECUTIVE STYLE HAIR.

WE THINK IT WILL TURN SILVER.

I FILLED OUT THE CONFIDENTIAL QUESTION-NAIRE ABOUT YOUR STYLE OF MANAGEMENT.

I HOPE IT'S USEFUL FOR THAT MANAGEMENT CLASS YOU'RE TAKING. ONLY YOUR INSTRUCTOR SEES THOSE, RIGHT?

RIGHT

I THINK I PLAYED THAT ABOUT RIGHT.

OOH, GOOD MARKS! AND IT SAYS HE TRUSTS ME TOO!

WE'LL BE GETTING A NEW "BUNGEE BOSS" SOMETIME TODAY.

HI-I'M-YOUR-NEW-BOSS-LET'S-CHANGE-EVERY-THING-BEFORE-I-GET-REASSIGNED-OOPS-TOO-LATE-GOODBYE.

SPROING

HE WAS LIKE A MENTOR TO ME.

I THINK HE MADE A DIFFERENCE.

INCOMING!

BOSSES

PLEASE DON'T PROMISE THE PRODUCT MANAGER MORE THAN WE CAN DELIVER.

WE NEED A TOTALLY NEW SOFTWARE INTERFACE IN ONE MONTH.

YOU GOT IT!

AND REWRITE THE OPERATING SYSTEM SO WE DOMINATE THE INDUSTRY.

CONCURRENT DEVELOPMENT.

CHECK

SUDDENLY I FEEL OMNIPOTENT.

I WANT ALL NEW HARDWARE, ANTI-GRAVITY PACKAGING, HOLOGRAPHIC AGENTS...

YAWN YAWN

CAN YOUR TEAM REALLY DO THAT IN A MONTH?

LET ME GET THEIR REACTION.

AAAGH!!

PESSIMISM WILL NOT LOOK GOOD ON YOUR PERFORMANCE REVIEW.

TWITCH

I FINISHED THE TECHNICAL RECOMMENDATION YOU REQUESTED.

AT FIRST I WAS MIFFED THAT YOU TOLD ME WHAT RECOMMENDATION YOU WANTED.

IT MADE ME FEEL USELESS AND WEAK.

BUT RATHER THAN DWELL ON MY POWERLESSNESS...

I DECIDED TO FIND JOY IN THE ONE DECISION I CAN MAKE.

I CHOSE A HELVETICA TYPE FONT.

AND I NEVER LOOKED BACK.

OH, SO THAT'S WHAT'S WRONG WITH IT.

I COACH AND I COACH, BUT THEY STILL WALK OUT OF HERE ALL RUBBER-LEGGED.

BOSSES

THIS BELL WILL IMPROVE YOUR MORALE.

YOU RING THE BELL WHENEVER YOU ACHIEVE A GOAL.

THEN YELL YOUR ACCOMPLISHMENT TO THE REST OF THE OFFICE

I KNOW IT SOUNDS CORNY, BUT THE BELL HAS WORKED AT OTHER COMPANIES.

DOES YOUR INFORMATION COME FROM THE BOSSES OF THOSE OTHER COMPANIES?

NO.
IT COMES FROM A MAGAZINE WHO INTERVIEWED THOSE BOSSES.

I'LL GO FIRST.
CLANG CLANG

I RESISTED KILLING MY BOSS WITH A STUPID BELL!!

I NEED SOME MANAGEMENT FIRE POWER.

THE VP OF MARKETING SAYS WE CAN'T USE THE VENDOR WE SELECTED...

LET ME WRITE THIS DOWN.

DO YOU WANT SOME PAPER?
NO, I'LL USE THIS TISSUE... OOPS.

ANYWAY, THE OTHER VENDOR CAN'T DELIVER.
OOPS.

I HAVE SOME NOTE PAPER.
NO, THIS IS FINE.
OOPS.

ALL YOU HAVE IS A BLOTCH ON A SCRAP.
IT'S MORE OF A REMINDER THAN A DETAILED NOTE.

HMM... IT'S NOT SO USEFUL WHEN I PUT IT WITH THE OTHERS.

BOSSES

LUNCH WITH A TOP EXECUTIVE

I HAVE THESE LUNCHES TO FIND OUT WHAT THE WORKERS ARE THINKING. YOU MAY SPEAK FREELY.

OKAY... IT SEEMS LIKE THE COMPANY IS LACKING LEADERSHIP AND DIRECTION. THE EXECUTIVES SQUELCH ALL INITIATIVE BY PUNISHING THOSE WHO TAKE RISKS AND VOICE OPINIONS.

YOU LEAVE ME LITTLE CHOICE BUT TO FLING THIS AU GRATIN POTATO AT YOUR FOREHEAD.

THIS IS URGENT. I NEED IT BY TOMORROW.

YOU'VE KNOWN ABOUT THIS FOR WEEKS. NOW I'LL HAVE TO WORK ALL NIGHT!

COULD YOU AT LEAST SAY SOMETHING THAT SOUNDS GRATEFUL?

I'M GLAD I'M ME!

I'VE GOT GOOD NEWS AND BAD NEWS.

THE BAD NEWS IS THAT HUGE COMPANIES LIKE US CAN'T COMPETE AGAINST SMALL, NIMBLE COMPANIES. THE GOOD NEWS IS THAT AT THIS RATE WE'LL BE THE SMALLEST COMPANY AROUND.

WHAT AM I DOING WRONG HERE?

WE'RE NUMBER ONE! WE'RE NUMBER ONE! YES!!

...BUT OUR PRIMARY VENDOR CAN'T DELIVER, SO...

I WONDER WHAT'S ON TV TONIGHT.

...SHOULD WE RISK A LAWSUIT OR BUILD A A PRODUCT THAT NOBODY ON EARTH WANTS?

DID HE ASK ME TO MAKE A CHOICE?

WILL IT BE A REQUEST FOR INFORMATION OR AN IMPRACTICAL SOLUTION?

LET'S DO BOTH!

IT'S TIME TO GO HOME. THAT MEANS...

HI

RIGHT ON SCHEDULE.

WAIT. LET ME GUESS WHY YOU'RE HERE.

YOU WANT TO DISCUSS A DOCUMENT THAT'S BEEN ON YOUR DESK FOR A MONTH.

IT'S SOMETHING THAT COULD EASILY WAIT UNTIL TOMORROW.

BUT YOU'LL INSIST THAT I HANDLE IT NOW BECAUSE YOU'RE A SOCIOPATH.

WRONG. I MAJORED IN ANTHROPOLOGY.

BUT THAT WAS A SPOOKILY ACCURATE GUESS ABOUT THE DOCUMENT.

DID YOU KNOW THAT TWENTY PERCENT OF ALL MICROFLEEMS ARE SUBRADIANTE?

UH-OH. THE BOSS HAS LATCHED ONTO SOME OBSCURE ENGINEERING FACT.

THIS IS GOING TO BE PAINFUL.

JUST THINK OF THE IMPLICATIONS. IT MEANS EIGHTY PERCENT OF MICROFLEEMS ARE NOT SUBRADIANTE.

MAYBE I CAN HIDE UNDER THE DESK UNTIL THIS BLOWS OVER.

DON'T YOU THINK IT'S FASCINATING? I MEAN, WHAT WITH THE IMPLICATIONS AND ALL...

OKAY, OKAY. I ACKNOWLEDGE YOUR INCREDIBLE GRASP OF TECHNOLOGY ISSUES.

IT ALMOST MAKES ME CURIOUS WHAT A MICROFLEEM IS.

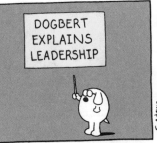

DOGBERT EXPLAINS LEADERSHIP

LEADERS START THEIR CAREERS AS MORONS.

THEY ARE DRAWN TO MEETINGS LIKE MOTHS TO A PORCH LIGHT.

THE SUCCESSFUL MORON WILL HAVE A VERY HIGH BLADDER-TO-BRAIN RATIO.

BRAIN

BLADDER

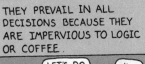

THEY PREVAIL IN ALL DECISIONS BECAUSE THEY ARE IMPERVIOUS TO LOGIC OR COFFEE.

LET'S DO IT MY WAY!

OKAY!

THESE QUALITIES ARE PERCEIVED AS LEADERSHIP.

YOU'RE PROMOTED!

AFTER SEVERAL PROMOTIONS THEIR JOB TENDS TO MATCH THEIR TALENTS.

I AWARD YOU THIS AWARD.

CONCLUSION: LEADERSHIP IS NATURE'S WAY OF REMOVING MORONS FROM THE PRODUCTIVE FLOW.

DO YOU HAVE A MINUTE?

UH-OH, IT'S TOUCHY-FEELY STUFF.

WHAT'S GOING TO HAPPEN TO OUR DEPARTMENT? THE RUMORS ARE FLYING.

WHAT HAVE YOU HEARD?

RUMOR HAS IT THAT FLYING LIZARDS FROM THE PLANET ZORB WILL BUY THE COMPANY.

THEY PLAN TO TURN THE EMPLOYEES INTO GIANT CORN DOGS ON STICKS.

DON'T WORRY ABOUT RUMORS. IT'S BUSINESS AS USUAL FOR NOW.

GULP

I THINK I HANDLED THAT PRETTY WELL.

ARE YOU SURE THIS WILL IMPRESS THE ZORBIANS?

I HEAR THEY LIKE TEAM PLAYERS.

BOSSES

SON-OF-A-BOSS

YOU HAVE TO MAKE OUR PRODUCT SO SIMPLE THAT MY MOM COULD USE IT.

IT'S ALREADY SO SIMPLE A HAMSTER COULD USE IT. HOW MUCH DUMBER IS YOUR MOM?

MAYBE WE SHOULD LEAVE MY MOM OUT OF THIS.

MY MOM IS A PHYSICIST.

OUR NEW E-MAIL MONITORING SYSTEM SHOWS THAT YOU SENT A PERSONAL MESSAGE LAST WEEK.

COINCIDENTALLY, THE NEW ALICE MONITORING SYSTEM DETECTS TWENTY HOURS OF UNPAID OVERTIME.

ACCORDING TO THE MANUAL, PRODUC- TIVITY WILL SOAR NOW.

BEEP... BEEP... BOOP... NOW DETECTING CLUELESSNESS IN THE VICINITY.

I SUGGEST THAT YOU DEAL WITH THE ISSUE ON A GOING FORWARD BASIS.

THANKS FOR RULING OUT TIME TRAVEL. YOU'RE USUALLY NOT THAT HELPFUL.

ARE YOU SAYING HE UNDERSTANDS THE CONCEPT OF "TIME" NOW?

OR HE JUST GOT LUCKY ON THIS ONE.

ALICE, I'M SENDING YOU TO ELBONIA TO INSPECT OUR FACTORY.

FILL OUT A TRIP JUSTIFICATION FORM FOR MY APPROVAL.

SO, I NEED YOUR APPROVAL TO DO WHAT YOU TOLD ME TO DO?

IT WILL NOT BE UNREASONABLY WITHHELD.

DILBERT *Gives You the Business*

BOSSES

OUR NEW VP SAYS HE HAS AN "OPEN DOOR POLICY." LET'S CHECK IT OUT.

KNOCK KNOCK

HI HO. NOTHING IMPORTANT. WE JUST WANTED TO DROP IN.

THIS OPEN DOOR POLICY IS GREAT. OUR LAST VP WAS ALOOF.

ARE THOSE SOURBALLS?

LOOK AT ALL THE FURNITURE IN HERE!

I CALL COUCH!

IS THERE SOMETHING I CAN DO FOR YOU?

WELL...SOMETIMES OUR CUBICLES ARE TOO HOT.

COULD YOU HAVE SOMEBODY LOOK INTO IT?

BOY, THOSE SOURBALLS SURE LULL YOU INTO A FALSE SENSE OF SECURITY.

THE MAN IS LIKE A HUGE INSINCERE SPIDER.

WHAT WE NEED IS MORE COMMUNICATION BETWEEN MANAGEMENT AND...WHATEVER YOU ARE.

SO, ONCE A MONTH I'LL HAVE "OPEN DOOR DAY."

YOU CAN DROP BY AND WHINE ABOUT ANYTHING YOU WANT.

I'LL LISTEN WITH A CONCERNED EXPRESSION LIKE THIS.

THEN I'LL EXPLAIN WHY EVERYTHING IS FINE JUST THE WAY IT IS.

THEN, MORALE WILL IMPROVE, PROFITS WILL SKYROCKET AND MY STOCK OPTIONS WILL MAKE ME RICH!!

MAY I MAKE SOME OBSERVATIONS ABOUT YOUR PLAN?

UH... FORGET IT.

DO YOU NOTICE HOW CONCERNED I LOOK?

I'LL NEED A LETTER OF REFERENCE TO APPLY FOR A JOB IN ANOTHER DIVISION.

NO PROBLEM.

... FOR A MAN OF HIS HYGIENE, HE DOESN'T STEAL AS MUCH AS YOU'D THINK. I SUSPECT HE'S ON DRUGS.

AND THEN HE SAYS YOU'RE PRONE TO ANGER AND DENIAL. IS THAT TRUE?

NO!!

THE COMPANY HAS DECIDED TO OUTSOURCE ALL OF THE FUNCTIONS THAT WE'RE NOT ANY GOOD AT.

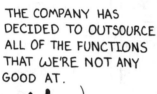

Yippee!

Yay!

WHEN'S YOUR LAST DAY?

UH-OH...THEY'RE NOT GOOD AT KNOWING WHAT THEY'RE NOT GOOD AT...

SO, YOU IGNORED MY RECOMMENDATION AND BOUGHT A LOW-COST SYSTEM THAT'S TOTALLY INADEQUATE...

YOU COMPENSATED FOR THIS BLUNDER BY MAKING IT PART OF MY OBJECTIVES TO MAKE THE SYSTEM WORK...

YOU'LL GET A BONUS FOR SAVING MONEY. I'LL GET FIRED, THUS SAVING MORE MONEY AND EARNING YOU ANOTHER BONUS.

I'M ON A ROLL.

IT HAS COME TO MY ATTENTION THAT 40% OF YOUR SICK DAYS ARE ON FRIDAYS AND MONDAYS. THIS IS UNACCEPTABLE.

HA HA HA!!! THAT'S A GOOD ONE!!!

PLEASE TELL ME HE WAS KIDDING.

WELCOME TO HELL, KID.

ALICE, OUR RECORDS SHOW THAT YOU HAVEN'T TAKEN A VACATION ALL YEAR.

COMPANY POLICY REQUIRES YOU TO USE YOUR VACATION DAYS.

HOW?? YOU TOLD ME TO WORK SEVEN DAYS A WEEK TO PREPARE THE PROJECT FOR YOUR BOSS'S YEAR-END REVIEW.

DO YOU WANT ME TO MEET THE ARTIFICIAL PROJECT TARGET OR THE ARTIFICIAL VACATION TARGET?

HELLO!!! THESE ARE MUTUALLY EXCLUSIVE GOALS!!! HELLO!!!

OOH... SORRY. I USUALLY JUST THINK THAT LAST PART IN SILENT FRUSTRATION.

MOVING RIGHT ALONG... KUDOS TO WALLY FOR USING ALL OF HIS VACATION DAYS AHEAD OF SCHEDULE.

GET OVER IT, ALICE. WE CAN'T ALL BE SUPERSTARS.

HERE'S THE ANALYSIS YOU ASKED FOR... I WORKED ALL NIGHT.

BUT YOU SAID THIS WAS VITAL FOR YOUR MEETING TODAY SO I KNOW IT WAS WORTH THE EFFORT.

THIS IS EXCELLENT WORK, ALICE.

A RARE COMPLIMENT; IT WAS ALL WORTH-WHILE.

MMM

I'LL USE IT AS BACKUP MATERIAL.

BACKUP?!! NOBODY LOOKS AT BACKUP MATERIAL!

I'M GOING TO GRAB YOUR POINTY HAIR, YANK YOU OUT OF THAT CHEAP SUIT AND FLING YOUR NAKED BODY DOWN THE HALL.

SHE'S ALWAYS IRRITABLE THE WEEK BEFORE HER PERFORMANCE REVIEW CYCLE.

HER DISTANCE IMPROVED THIS YEAR.

OW

IT'S TIME FOR MY ANNUAL INSPIRATIONAL TALK!

WE MUST WORK TWICE AS HARD, OR THE COMPETITION WILL CRUSH US!

I WANT YOU TO FEEL AFRAID TWENTY-FOUR HOURS A DAY!

QUESTION: WOULDN'T THAT LOWER THE QUALITY OF OUR LIVES?

SEEMS LIKE IT MIGHT

I'M TOO AFRAID TO WORK HERE NOW. I WONDER IF OUR COMPETITORS ARE HIRING.

QUESTION: SHOULD WE CONTINUE TO BE AFRAID OF OUR OWN MANAGEMENT'S INCOMPETENCE?

LET'S COMPROMISE. I'LL CUT THE MEETING SHORT IF YOU'LL ALL AGREE TO FEEL WORSE IN SOME WAY.

NOW I REMEMBER WHY I ONLY INSPIRE THEM ONCE A YEAR.

THANKS FOR YOUR TIME, DILBERT. IT'S ALWAYS GOOD TO GET THE TECHNICAL PERSPECTIVE.

HEY, IT'S LUNCHTIME. WOULD YOU LIKE TO JOIN ME IN THE CAFETERIA?

OOH... NO, I COULDN'T DO THAT.

I'M ON THE MANAGEMENT TRACK, SO I CAN'T BE SEEN EATING LUNCH WITH YOU.

IF I'M SEEN WITH AN ORDINARY EMPLOYEE THEN PEOPLE WILL THINK I'M ORDINARY.

I'D LIKE TO EAT WITH THE SENIOR EXECUTIVES, BUT OF COURSE THEY DON'T WANT TO BE SEEN WITH ME.

SO I'VE PERFECTED A METHOD OF SLIPPING QUIETLY AWAY AT LUNCH TIME.

THE SCARY PART IS THAT SOMEDAY THAT MAN WILL BE MY BOSS.

YOUR EXPENSE REPORT WAS REJECTED BY ACCOUNTING.

WHY?

BECAUSE THE EMPTINESS OF THEIR SHALLOW LIVES MAKES THEM WANT TO HURT OTHERS IN ORDER TO VALIDATE THEIR PATHETIC EXISTENCE.

CAN YOU HELP ME CLEAR THIS UP?

TO BE HONEST, I'M KINDA BUYING IN TO THEIR PHILOSOPHY.

THE COMPANY IS A BILLION DOLLARS BELOW ITS EARNINGS PROJECTIONS.

FROM NOW ON, ONLY THE MANAGERS AT MY LEVEL OR ABOVE MAY EAT DONUTS AT COMPANY MEETINGS.

THIS WON'T BE EASY FOR ANY OF US. HECK, I DON'T EVEN KNOW IF I CAN EAT THIS MANY DONUTS.

I'M ASKING EVERYBODY TO QUANTIFY THEIR CONTRIBUTIONS TO REVENUE. YOUR PAY WILL DEPEND ON IT.

I REALIZE THIS IS HARD TO QUANTIFY BECAUSE YOU'RE DESIGNING FUTURE PRODUCTS BUT...

HERE YOU GO.

A BILLION DOLLARS? IT'S AS IF YOU CYNICALLY BELIEVE WE CAN'T TRACK THESE NUMBERS.

THAT CROSSED MY MIND.

DILBERT, I NEED YOU TO STOP EVERYTHING AND DO THIS EMERGENCY BUDGET EXERCISE.

ESTIMATE THE BUDGET IMPACT OF REPLACING ALL THE ENGINEERS WITH DECORATIVE PLANTS.

LATER, I'LL SUMMARIZE EVERYBODY'S INPUTS INTO A BULLET POINT, LIKE "OXYGEN IS GOOD."

WOULD THESE BE RENTED PLANTS?

I SUMMARIZED THE BUDGET IMPACTS ON SIX HUNDRED PROJECTS WITH THOSE THREE BULLET POINTS.

"—OXYGEN IS GOOD
—COMPETITION IS BAD
—I LIKE JELLO"

DO YOU THINK IT'S TOO DETAILED FOR THE SENIOR EXECUTIVES?

TAKE OUT THE "COMPETITION" ONE.

MY BOSS TOLD ME TO BUY A BUNCH OF EQUIPMENT WE DON'T NEED.

THAT WAY OUR BUDGET WON'T GET CUT NEXT YEAR.

I'M SO PROUD OF YOU, SON.

HOW DO YOU SAY THAT WITH A STRAIGHT FACE?

I TRY TO IMAGINE YOU AS A NAVY SEAL.

THIS 3-D COLORED PIE CHART SHOWS AN UNEXPLAINED RISE IN EXPENSES.

?

YOU EACH GET A BINDER OF COLORED PIE CHARTS SO YOU CAN HELP FIND THE CAUSE OF OUR RISING EXPENSES.

HOW MUCH DO COLOR COPIES COST?

I THINK I SEE IT!

IT'S NOT THE "MAGIC EYE," DOOFUS.

WE'LL HAVE TO ELIMINATE A FEW STEPS IN ORDER TO HIT THE MARKET WINDOW.

I THINK WE CAN GET RID OF MARKET RESEARCH AND TECHNICAL TESTING. THEY'RE BASICALLY "OVERHEAD."

GONE! NOW WE'LL HIT THE WINDOW!

...LIKE A BIRD.

I'D LIKE YOU ALL TO MEET OUR NEW VICE PRESIDENT IN CHARGE OF COST CONTAINMENT.

MY FIRST PRIORITY IS TO REDUCE OUR SPIRALING EXPENSES FOR OFFICE SUPPLIES.

FROM NOW ON, YOUR SUPPLY CABINET WILL BE LOCKED.

THE ONLY KEY WILL BE UNDER THE CONTROL OF YOUR BITTER AND INEFFICIENT SECRETARY.

QUESTIONS?

I AM ONLY AN INTERN SO PLEASE EXCUSE THIS NAIVE QUESTION...

I'VE NOTICED THAT THE EMPLOYEES ARE ALL DISPIRITED HOLLOW SHELLS, MANAGEMENT IS RANDOM AND OUR PRODUCTS ARE SHODDY.

HOW ARE YOU GOING TO SOLVE THAT BY MAKING IT HARD TO GET SUPPLIES?

I THOUGHT YOU SAID THEY LIKE HONESTY.

ASK HOW MUCH HE'S PAID. IT SHOWS YOU CARE.

IT'S TIME TO DELEGATE.

DILBERT, I WANT YOU TO GIVE ME A NEW CASH FLOW ESTIMATE FOR YOUR PROJECT.

OKAY, FINE.

WHEN WILL I GET IT?

WHEN DO YOU NEED IT?

AS SOON AS POSSIBLE!

OKAY.

AND WHEN DO YOU THINK THAT WILL BE?

I USUALLY WAIT A FEW DAYS TO SEE IF YOU CHANGE YOUR MIND.

THEN I'LL GIVE YOU LAST YEAR'S CASH FLOW AS A TEST TO SEE IF YOU READ IT.

THE MORE EXPERIENCE THEY GET, THE WORSE THEY ARE.

DOGBERT IS A CREATIVITY CONSULTANT

WE DON'T NEED ANY OF YOUR "INTUITION" MUMBO JUMBO. WE NEED QUANTITATIVE DATA!

THE ONLY WAY TO MAKE DECISIONS IS TO PULL NUMBERS OUT OF THE AIR, CALL THEM "ASSUMPTIONS," AND CALCULATE THE NET PRESENT VALUE.

OF COURSE, YOU HAVE TO USE THE RIGHT DISCOUNT RATE, OTHERWISE IT'S MEANINGLESS.

GO AWAY.

DILBERT, GO DOWN TO THE ACCOUNTING DEPARTMENT AND FIND OUT WHAT THESE FIGURES MEAN.

GULP

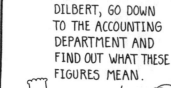

NO... P-PLEASE... THEY AREN'T EVEN HUMAN THERE!!!

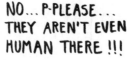

I DON'T LIKE HIM.

SURPRISE.

THIS MUST BE THE COMPANY ACCOUNTING DEPARTMENT.

I... I NEED TO ASK SOME QUESTIONS ABOUT THIS B-BUDGET REPORT.

IS THIS A BAD TIME FOR YOU?

ALWAYS.

FOOL! WHY HAVE YOU COME TO THE ACCOUNTING DEPARTMENT?!!

UH... I HAD SOME QUESTIONS, SIR... MA'AM... ER, SIR?

ARE YOU A MAN OR WOMAN?

IN ACCOUNTING, IT DOESN'T REALLY MATTER.

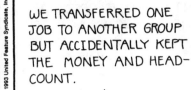

I FOUND A TYPO IN THE BUDGET SPREAD-SHEET... IT'S TOO LATE TO FIX IT.

WE TRANSFERRED ONE JOB TO ANOTHER GROUP BUT ACCIDENTALLY KEPT THE MONEY AND HEAD-COUNT.

...SO, WE STILL PAY YOU BUT YOU AREN'T ALLOWED TO DO WORK.

THIS IS THE HAPPIEST DAY OF MY LIFE.

PROJECT STATUS

DUE TO BUDGET CUTS, OUR NEW PRODUCT WILL HAVE NO USER INTERFACE.

OUR TARGET MARKET IS PEOPLE WHO ARE TOO SHY TO RETURN PRODUCTS.

IS IT A BAD SIGN IF YOU SPEND THE DAY WONDERING WHY THERE ARE NO LAWS AGAINST WHAT YOU DO FOR A LIVING?

HERE ARE MY BUDGET ESTIMATES FOR THE YEAR.

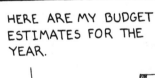

THANKS TO MANAGEMENT BUNGLING AND INDE-CISION, I PLAN TO USE NO CAPITAL FOR SEVERAL MONTHS FOLLOWED BY A RECKLESS YEAR-END ORGY OF ACQUISITION.

IS THAT WHAT YOU WERE LOOKING FOR?

TELL ME AGAIN WHAT "CAPITAL" IS.

DILBERT, I WANT YOU TO HELP SUSAN PUT THE DEPARTMENT BUDGET TOGETHER.

BUDGET?!

NO, PLEASE! I'LL BE BRANDED FOR LIFE. THE OTHER ENGINEERS WILL SPIT ON ME.

DARN, HIS GUARD IS UP.

I'LL HAVE TO WEAR A RAINCOAT TO WORK!

BUDGETING AND ACCOUNTING

DILBERT IS ASSIGNED TO PREPARE THE BUDGET.

YOU'LL HAVE TO LEARN OUR BUDGET SYSTEM.

IT WAS DEVELOPED 400 YEARS AGO BY A CRAZED MONK WHO SEALED HIMSELF IN A WINE CASK.

UNFORTUNATELY, WE STILL HAVE HIM.

HEY, I'VE GOT ANOTHER IDEA.

THE OTHER ENGINEERS SHUN ME BECAUSE I'M ASSIGNED TO WORK ON THE BUDGET.

SHUN

THEY KNOW I COULD POUNCE ANY MOMENT AND ASK INANE HYPOTHETICAL BUDGET QUESTIONS.

SHUN

WHAT IF YOU ONLY HAD HALF AS MUCH ELECTRICITY NEXT YEAR?

TOO LATE. I SHUNNED YOU.

HEY, "DIL-BUTT," I HEAR THEY GOT YOU DOING BUDGET WORK NOW.

HA HA! IT MUST BE REALLY EXCITING WORK. I MEAN, GOSH, MAKING ALL THOSE NUMBERS ADD UP.

HA HA! I'M GLAD I HAVE A REAL JOB!

NOT ANYMORE.

CLICK

DOGBERT THE C.E.O.

I'VE DECIDED TO MANIPULATE OUR STOCK PRICE FOR PERSONAL GAIN.

I'LL SPIN OFF A FEW DIVISIONS, BUY BACK SOME OF OUR STOCK AND ANNOUNCE MASSIVE BUDGET CUTS.

UM...DO YOU EVEN KNOW WHAT PRODUCTS WE MAKE?

HOW WOULD THAT BE RELEVANT?

THE BUDGET TRAP

I NEED A QUICK ESTIMATE FOR HOW MUCH YOUR NEXT PROJECT WILL COST, WALLY.

HOW SHOULD I KNOW? YOU HAVEN'T EVEN TOLD ME WHAT MY NEXT PROJECT IS.

THAT'S OKAY. I ONLY NEED A ROUGH ESTIMATE FOR PLANNING PURPOSES.

I SEE WHERE THIS IS GOING. YOU'RE GOING TO TURN MY WILD GUESS INTO A BUDGET. LATER I'LL BE BLAMED WHEN IT'S WRONG.

NO, NO. I WON'T HOLD YOU TO THESE NUMBERS.

WELL...OKAY, LET'S SAY TWO MILLION DOLLARS.

OOH... CAN'T AFFORD THAT. I'LL PUT YOU DOWN FOR TWENTY THOUSAND DOLLARS.

ONE YEAR LATER...

YOU'RE WAY OVER BUDGET. CAN YOU SHOW ME THE CAUSE?

IT DEPENDS. CAN MIRRORS REFLECT YOUR IMAGE?

HOW MUCH BUDGET DO I HAVE FOR MY PROJECT?

I CAN'T TELL YOU.

IF YOU KNEW WHAT YOUR BUDGET WAS, YOU'D SPEND IT ALL.

CAN YOU AT LEAST TELL ME WHAT OUR COMPANY STRATEGY IS?

NO, I DON'T WANT YOU TO LOSE HOPE.

I HAVE TO CUT JANITOR EXPENSES. DO YOU THINK I'LL HAVE ANY HR ISSUES IF I MAKE EMPLOYEES EMPTY THEIR OWN TRASH?

WE'LL SOFTEN THE BAD NEWS BY SIMULTANEOUSLY INTRODUCING A NEW EMPLOYEE FITNESS PROGRAM...

OKAY, EVERYBODY, IT'S TIME TO TRASHERCISE!!!

IF IT'S OKAY, I'LL HOLD ONTO MY SOUL WHILE I VISIT THE ACCOUNTING DEPARTMENT.

SOUL CHECK

I CAME TO ANSWER YOUR QUESTIONS ABOUT MY EXPENSE REPORT.

TAKE A SEAT.

I DON'T LIKE THE WAY THIS IS STARTING.

DILBERT'S EXPENSE VOUCHER

WHAT ARE YOU TRYING TO PULL?? DO YOU THINK WE'RE IDIOTS IN ACCOUNTING?!!

NO, I SWEAR, I THINK YOU'RE SMART BUT SADISTIC TROLLS WITH MANY HUMANOID CHARACTERISTICS.

APPARENTLY THERE WAS NO RIGHT ANSWER.

DILBERT'S EXPENSE VOUCHER

YOU SPENT NEARLY $10 PER DAY ON MEALS DURING YOUR TRIP.

THE TRAVEL GUIDELINES REQUIRE YOU TO STUN A PIGEON WITH YOUR BRIEFCASE ON THE WAY TO THE HOTEL THEN FRY IT UP ON YOUR TRAVEL IRON.

I TRIED...BUT IT WAS TAKING SO LONG.

TRY THE "WOOL" SETTING.

DILBERT IS TRAPPED IN THE BOWELS OF ACCOUNTING

I UNDERSTAND YOU HAVE DILBERT IN THERE. FREE HIM, OR ELSE...

ELSE WHAT?

OR ELSE I WILL PUT THIS CAP ON MY HEAD BACKWARDS! YOUR LITTLE HARDWIRED ACCOUNTING BRAIN WILL EXPLODE JUST LOOKING AT IT.

WHAT WAS THAT POPPING SOUND?

A PARADIGM SHIFTING WITHOUT A CLUTCH.

I'VE BEEN HIRED BY THE FINANCE DEPARTMENT TO HELP CUT SPENDING.

I'LL BE STUDYING YOUR EVERY MOVE AND LOOKING FOR WASTE AND INEFFICIENCY.

THOSE WORDS IN BOLDFACE LOOK LIKE THEY'RE SUCKING UP THE OL' ELECTRICITY.

I'M FROM THE FINANCE DEPARTMENT. I'M HERE TO REDUCE COSTS.

IT MIGHT SEEM LIKE ALL I DO IS COME UP WITH SHORT-SIGHTED WAYS TO SAVE MONEY WHILE MAKING YOUR JOB HARDER. BUT THERE'S ANOTHER SIDE TO THIS STORY.

AND THAT WOULD BE...?

I FORGET.

THE FINANCE DEPARTMENT HAS ANALYZED YOUR COMPUTING NEEDS AND DECIDED TO GIVE YOU A 286 PC.

THAT SHOULD BE SUFFICIENT FOR THE 3D-RENDERING YOU NEED TO DO.

BESIDES, HOW MANY TIMES ARE YOU GOING TO DO 3D-RENDERING IN YOUR CAREER?

ONCE, IF I HURRY.

HERE'S YOUR LATEST BUDGET CUTS. BUT PLEASE DON'T KILL THE MESSENGER FROM FINANCE, HA HA!!

I RECOMMENDED A 20% CUT. A QUICK GLANCE AROUND THE ROOM TELLS ME YOU'RE NOT ON THE SUCCESS VECTOR ANYHOO, SO NOTHING LOST.

TOUGH ROOM.

GOOD NEWS ON YOUR BUDGETS. I DID SOME RECALCULATING LAST NIGHT.

I FOUND A WAY TO GIVE MORE MONEY TO EVERY PROJECT WITHOUT INCREASING THE TOTAL BUDGET FOR PROJECTS!

QUESTION: DOES YOUR NEW WAY INVOLVE POOR MATH SKILLS?

IGNORE THE SKEPTIC.

HEY, I HAVE A SUGGESTION!

?

MAYBE YOU COULD RECALCULATE OUR SALARY BUDGET NEXT.

AND WHEN WAS THE LAST TIME YOU RECALCULATED OUR VACATION DAYS?

I CALCULATE THAT WE HAVE AN HOUR LEFT FOR THIS MEETING. BUT I'M INTERESTED IN YOUR CALCULATION.

I THINK WE GOT GREEDY WHEN WE ASKED IF HE HAD CHANGE FOR A FIVE.

HERE'S THE GOAL THAT WILL MOTIVATE YOU FOR THE NEXT YEAR.

"BUILD A GLOBAL SATELLITE NETWORK. BUDGET: $12,000."

MOTIVATION FEELS MUCH DIFFERENT FROM WHAT I IMAGINED.

I WAS EXPECTING A LIGHT, ENERGETIC FEELING.

BUT IT'S MORE LIKE BEING PINNED UNDER A BURNING COUCH.

WHOO! I'M GETTING DIZZY.

I'D BETTER LIE DOWN UNTIL THE MOTIVATION WEARS OFF.

HE'S GOING TO BE TROUBLE DURING THE NEXT ROUND OF BUDGET CUTS.

© 1998 United Feature Syndicate, Inc.

WE NEED TO BOOST OUR RETURN-ON-ASSETS RATIO.

LET'S ELIMINATE THE SECURITY DEPARTMENT. THAT WOULD CUT EXPENSES WHILE ALLOWING FOR A BRISK REDUCTION IN ASSETS.

WHEN ARE YOU PLANNING TO TELL HIM YOU WERE JOKING?

AFTER I FURNISH MY DEN.

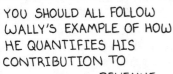

YOU SHOULD ALL FOLLOW WALLY'S EXAMPLE OF HOW HE QUANTIFIES HIS CONTRIBUTION TO REVENUE.

BASICALLY, I ASSUMED MY PROJECT WOULD FAIL WITHOUT ME. THEREFORE ALL THE REVENUE IT GENERATES CAN BE ATTRIBUTED TO ME.

AREN'T WE ALL ON THE SAME PROJECT?

YES, BUT EVIDENTLY WE'RE NOT ALL EQUALLY VALUABLE.

I LIKE TO CON PEOPLE. AND I LIKE TO INSULT PEOPLE.

IF YOU COMBINE CON AND INSULT, YOU GET "CONSULT."

I'M HERE TO CONSULT YOU.

IT SOUNDS EXPENSIVE AND DEMEANING. ... OKAY.

I HIRED THE "DOGBERT CONSULTING COMPANY" TO LEAD THE PROJECT BECAUSE NONE OF YOU IS BRIGHT ENOUGH.

AND YOU ALL HAVE BAD ATTITUDES FOR NO APPARENT REASON; THAT'S NO WAY TO BE A LEADER.

SHALL WE GO AROUND THE TABLE AND INTRODUCE OURSELVES?

I DON'T GET CHUMMY WITH THE LOCALS.

I'VE ASKED DOGBERT TO HELP US GET RID OF OUR MOST TROUBLESOME CUSTOMERS.

GRRR

TEN PERCENT OF YOUR CUSTOMERS ACCOUNT FOR NINETY PERCENT OF YOUR SERVICE COSTS. THEY MUST BE ELIMINATED.

IS THAT THE SAME GROUP OF CUSTOMERS WHO ACTUALLY USE OUR PRODUCT?

PLUS THE ONES WHO WERE INJURED UNPACKING IT.

RING

HELLO, I'M A RAT.

THIS IS A CONSULTING COMPANY. WE'LL PAY YOU $200,000 PER YEAR TO WORK FOR US.

I'M MORE INTERESTED IN INVESTMENT BANKING.

*#!☺ JOB MARKET.

COME WORK FOR OUR CONSULTING FIRM AND YOU WILL GET THIS BUSHEL OF MONEY.

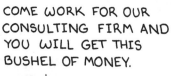

ALL WE WANT IN RETURN IS TWENTY HOURS OF WORK EACH DAY...

...WITH CLIENTS WHO HATE YOU FOR A VARIETY OF GOOD REASONS.

AT LEAST THERE'S NO TRAVEL, RIGHT?

RATBERT THE CONSULTANT

AS OUR NEWEST PARTNER, YOU'LL GET THE LEAST DESIRABLE ASSIGNMENTS.

WE'LL LOAD YOU IN THE CONSULTANT CANNON, SHOOT YOU TO THE CLIENT'S SITE AND MONITOR YOUR PROGRESS.

THE WINDOW IS MORE TO THE LEFT.

THE CLIENT IS MORE TO THE RIGHT.

RATBERT THE CONSULTANT

I'M MAKING $200,000 PER YEAR!

APPARENTLY THAT'S ALL I KNOW.

THANKS TO MY CONSULTING JOB, I'M WEALTHIER THAN YOU.

AND I'M CUTER, OBVIOUSLY. THE ONLY THING LEFT IS PERSONALITY.

SHOULDN'T YOU BE SPREADING DISEASE SOMEWHERE?

THREE FOR THREE! YES!!

WHY SHOULD I HIRE YOU AS MY BUSINESS CONSULTANT?

I HAVE CREDIBILITY BECAUSE I DON'T WORK FOR YOUR COMPANY. NO SMART PERSON WOULD WORK HERE FULL-TIME.

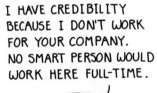

I WORK HERE FULL-TIME.

SORRY. I'LL TRY TO SPEAK SLOW-ER.

MY FEE FOR BUSINESS CON-SULTING IS $200 AN HOUR.

FAIR ENOUGH.

I'LL SPEND THE DAY QUESTIONING YOUR EMPLOYEES TO IDEN-TIFY PROBLEM AREAS.

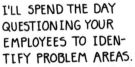

LATER

IT'S UNANIMOUS. THEY'RE UNDER-PAID AND ALL THE PROBLEMS ARE YOUR FAULT, "LARD HEAD."

DILBERT *Gives You the Business*

CONSULTING

YOUR NEW LOGO MIGHT LOOK LIKE A SIMPLE COFFEE STAIN, BUT WHAT DOES THE IMAGE SAY ABOUT YOU?

WE'RE SLOPPY AND UNIMAGINATIVE?

WE GIVE LOTS OF MONEY TO CONSULTANTS AND GET LITTLE IN RETURN?

WOW. THIS IS ALMOST TOO GOOD.

OOH OOH! HOW ABOUT "OUR OPINIONS DON'T MATTER"?

I'VE SEEN HIM BEFORE.

I'M A "BLAME CONSULTANT."

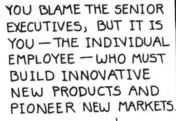

FOR A LARGE FEE I WILL TELL THE WORKERS THAT THE PROBLEMS IN THE COMPANY ARE THEIR FAULT, NOT YOURS. IT'S THE LATEST MANAGEMENT FAD.

WON'T THEY SEE RIGHT THROUGH THAT?

IS THAT MY FAULT??!

DOGBERT IS HIRED AS A BLAME CONSULTANT.

THE COMPANY'S PROBLEMS ARE YOUR FAULT, WILLY.

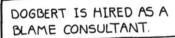

YOU BLAME THE SENIOR EXECUTIVES, BUT IT IS YOU — THE INDIVIDUAL EMPLOYEE — WHO MUST BUILD INNOVATIVE NEW PRODUCTS AND PIONEER NEW MARKETS.

BUT I'M JUST A WORD PROCESSOR. I WAS HIRED TO TYPE.

I'VE SEEN YOUR TYPING. THAT STINKS TOO.

DOGBERT IS HIRED AS A BLAME CONSULTANT.

THE COMPANY'S WOES ARE YOUR FAULT, NOT SENIOR MANAGEMENTS!

DO YOU REALIZE HOW MUCH YOU COULD GAIN PERSONALLY BY MAKING THE COMPANY A SUCCESS?

I WOULD GET A NICE PLAQUE IN A PLASTIC FRAME.

YEAH... I WAS HOPING YOU DIDN'T KNOW.

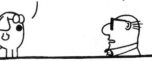

CONSULTING

AS YOUR CONSULTANT, I RECOMMEND THE "CAN-O-MATIC" TO REDUCE STAFF LEVELS.

DISGUISED AS A RESTROOM STALL, THE CAN-O-MATIC RANDOMLY FIRES PEOPLE BY SLAPPING A PINK SLIP ON THEIR BACKS AND CATAPULTING THEM OUT OF THE BUILDING.

BUT I WON'T GET TO SEE THE EXPRESSIONS ON THEIR FACES.

WELL, WE COULD FLING THEM PAST THE SECURITY CAMERAS HERE...

WE'VE GOT TO FOCUS MORE ON THE NEEDS OF OUR CUSTOMERS.

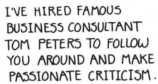

I'VE HIRED FAMOUS BUSINESS CONSULTANT TOM PETERS TO FOLLOW YOU AROUND AND MAKE PASSIONATE CRITICISM.

IS THIS QUALITY? ARE YOU TRULY FOCUSED ON THE CUSTOMER?

GREAT... HE'S A SPITTER.

DOGBERT THE CONSULTANT

I CAN GIVE YOU EXCELLENT ADVICE FOR $50,000 PER MONTH...

IF BUDGET IS A PROBLEM, I ALSO OFFER <u>BAD</u> ADVICE FOR THE LOW PRICE OF $45,000 PER MONTH.

THAT'S NOT A GOOD SIGN.

I SAVED A LOT OF MONEY BY HIRING A LOW-PRICED CONSULTANT.

THESE AREN'T THE BEST RECOMMENDATIONS IN THE WORLD, BUT THE PRICE WAS VERY REASONABLE.

I DON'T LIKE THIS ONE ABOUT ROLLING AROUND ON UNWASHED HAMBURGER PATTIES.

KEEP AN OPEN MIND.

ALTHOUGH YOUR COMPANY IS VERY PROFITABLE, I WOULDN'T BE MUCH OF A CONSULTANT IF I DIDN'T RECOMMEND CHANGES.

YOU RECOMMEND JAILING OUR OMBUDSMAN AND DECLARING MARTIAL LAW... MAKES SENSE.

THEN COULD I SHOOT EMPLOYEES WHO MAKE PERSONAL PHONE CALLS?

IT'S OKAY WITH ME.

AS A CONSULTANT, I'M OVERPAID EVEN IF I DO BAD WORK.

WHEREAS YOU'RE UNDERPAID EVEN IF YOU DO GOOD WORK.

IT'S FUNNY IF YOU THINK ABOUT IT.

I MIGHT HAVE A TERRIBLE JOB, BUT AT LEAST I DON'T HAVE ANY JOB SECURITY.

I CAN MAKE YOUR EMPLOYEES MORE CREATIVE AND SPIRITUALLY FULFILLED.

I USE MY SPECIAL BLEND OF POETRY AND DANCE TO TOUCH THEIR SOULS.

OKAY. YOU'RE HIRED.

THERE ONCE WAS A DOG WITH A HAT... WHO GOT PAID TO DANCE LIKE THAT...

HEY! MY SOUL JUST HEALED!

HAVE MY POEMS AND DANCES HEALED YOUR SOUL YET, ALICE? THE COMPANY CARES ABOUT YOUR TOTAL WELL BEING.

EXCUSE ME.

WE WANT MORE MONEY, NOT MORE DANCING DOGS!!! M-O-N-E-Y!!

SO YOU'RE SAYING THOSE PRIMAL SCREAMS ARE HEALTHY? CAN YOU TEACH ME TO DO IT?

HERE'S MY INVOICE—GO WILD.

DOGBERT THE CONSULTANT

I RECOMMEND THAT YOU REORGANIZE TO STRENGTHEN THE CORE COMPETENCY OF YOUR COMPANY.

AS LUCK WOULD HAVE IT, YOUR CORE COMPETENCY IS "GIVING MONEY TO CONSULTANTS."

I DON'T THINK THAT'S THE ONLY THING WE'RE GOOD AT.

IT DEPENDS ON IF YOU COUNT "WHINING."

MY CONSULTING PARTNER, RATBERT, WILL DEMONSTRATE HOW TO INFORM EMPLOYEES THAT THEIR JOBS WILL BE OUTSOURCED.

YOU'RE HISTORY. SCRAM.

BOOT

HOW DO I GET THEM ALL STOOPED OVER?

I RECOMMEND A PROGRAM OF VERY BAD ERGONOMICS.

HERE'S MY CONSULTING REPORT ON YOUR COMPANY.

I HAD NO INSIGHTS SO I BULKED IT UP BY ADDING WITTY ANALOGIES.

"HIS HEAD WAS LIKE A HOLLOW PUTTY BALL ATTACKED BY TWO POINTY DUST BUNNIES."

VIVID, ISN'T IT?

AS YOUR CONSULTANT I'LL BE ABLE TO UNLEASH RIGHT-BRAIN POTENTIAL IN YOUR EMPLOYEES.

THEY'LL LEARN TO FIND CREATIVE ANSWERS, NOT JUST RELY ON LEFT-BRAIN QUANTITATIVE ANALYSIS.

WHICH PART OF THE BRAIN DO WE USE FOR MEETINGS?

THAT WOULD BE THE STEM.

AS YOUR CONSULTANT I WILL UNLEASH THE CREATIVITY THAT THE COMPANY HAS SUPPRESSED.

WE'LL BEGIN WITH WORD ASSOCIATION. I'LL SAY A WORD THEN YOU EACH SAY WHAT POPS INTO YOUR HEAD.

CHAIR.

DONUT?

I SAY DONUT TOO.

I WAS GOING TO SAY DONUT.

DONUT

DOGBERT THE CREATIVITY CONSULTANT

THIS EXERCISE IS ESPECIALLY FOR THE MBAs IN THE COMPANY.

WHAT'S THE PAYBACK?

WHAP! WHAP! WHAP!

THERE'S NO RESEARCH TO SUPPORT THIS METHOD, BUT YOU GOTTA ADMIT IT FEELS RIGHT.

DOGBERT THE CONSULTANT

ONE WAY TO LOOK AT YOUR PROBLEM IS THAT NOBODY LIKES YOUR PRODUCTS.

BUT I DON'T KNOW HOW TO FIX THAT. SO I RECOMMEND FORMING INTERNAL BUSINESS UNITS TO BICKER WITH EACH OTHER.

WHY WOULD YOU RECOMMEND THAT?

WELL, I'D BE LYING IF I SAID I LIKED YOU.

WE'RE GOING TO FOLLOW THE ADVICE OF THE DOGBERT CONSULTING COMPANY AND FORM "BATTLIN' BUSINESS UNITS."

WE'LL SPEND MOST OF OUR TIME CROSS-CHARGING AND UNDERMINING THE OTHER BBU's.

A LITTLE COMPETITION IS HEALTHY.

WHATEVER YOU DO, DON'T TICK OFF THE JANITORIAL BBU.

DOGBERT THE CONSULTANT

WE TOOK YOUR ADVICE AND FORMED BUSINESS UNITS WITHIN THE COMPANY...

NOW WE SPEND ALL OF OUR TIME FIGHTING WITH EACH OTHER ABOUT WHO DOES WHAT.

WHAT EXACTLY DID YOU MEAN WHEN YOU SAID IT WOULD "GUARANTEE FUTURE BUSINESS"?

OH LOOK— MY CONTRACT JUST EXPIRED.

I HIRED RENOWNED PSYCHOLOGIST DOGBERT TO HELP US ACHIEVE PEAK PERFORMANCE IN TEAMWORK.

PEAK PERFORMANCE IS SOMEWHAT RELATIVE. YOU'RE A HIGHLY DYSFUNCTIONAL TEAM, SO WE MUST SET REALISTIC GOALS.

WHAT WOULD BE A REALISTIC GOAL FOR US?

I THINK I CAN POSTPONE CANNIBALISM.

DYSFUNCTIONAL TEAM...

I'D LIKE EVERYBODY TO TURN TO THE RIGHT AND SAY WHAT YOU ADMIRE ABOUT THAT PERSON.

I ADMIRE YOUR LEATHERY SKIN, ALICE.

I ADMIRE YOUR ABILITY TO FIGURE OUT WHICH SIDE IS YOUR RIGHT IN ONLY TWO TRIES.

I ADMIRE YOUR ABILITY TO GET PAID FOR THIS.

DESPITE THE FACT YOUR FACE SCARES CHILDREN, I ADMIRE YOUR CO-WORKERS.

I'M GOING TO TRY MY PAW AT BEING A CAREER COUNSELOR.

INSECURE PEOPLE WILL SEEK MY ADVICE AND I'LL TELL THEM TO BE MORE SELF-RELIANT.

THAT SOUNDS LAZY AND UNHELPFUL.

WOULD YOU WANT CAREER ADVICE FROM SOMEBODY WHO HAS TO WORK HARD?

CONSULTING

LET'S SEE... I'VE GOT MY CELLULAR PHONE, MY PAGER, PALM COMPUTER, PERSONAL ORGANIZER, WIRELESS MODEM...

YEAH, I'D SAY I'M PRETTY MUCH THE ENVY OF ENGINEERS EVERYWHERE... LOOKING GOOD... LOOKING GOOD...

WORDS ESCAPE ME...

HERE, I'LL FIRE UP THE OLD THESAURUS.

WALLY, I NOTICE THAT ALL YOU HAVE IS A PAGER AND A CALCULATOR WATCH.

UH-OH

THAT'S PATHETIC COMPARED TO MY VAST ARRAY OF PERSONAL ELECTRONICS. DO YOU YIELD TO MY TECHNICAL SUPERIORITY?

WHEN A MALE ENGINEER CHALLENGES ANOTHER FOR DOMINANCE OF THE PACK, THERE IS A BRIEF RITUALISTIC BATTLE RARELY SEEN BY OUTSIDERS.

STAY BACK, I'VE GOT A COMPASS!!

WIRELESS FAX!

AAGH!

MY VAST ARRAY OF PERSONAL TECHNOLOGY MAKES ME DOMINANT OVER THE LESS-EQUIPPED ENGINEERS.

I AM SUPERIOR TO THEM ALL... WITH THE POSSIBLE EXCEPTION OF...

TECHNO-BILL !!

LOOKS LIKE SOMEBODY JUST HAD A FAX.

PLEASE DON'T HURT ME, TECHNO-BILL!

MAKE YOUR MOVE.

MY ONLY CHANCE IS TO USE MY CELLULAR PHONE AND MODEM TO DIAL INTO HIS CONTROL MODULE AND SET OFF ALL HIS SYSTEMS.

FOOL! I HAVE AUTODIALING.

BEEP BEEP AAAGH! BZZZ BZZZZ BZZZ RRRING! DING

ENGINEERS

ENGINEERS

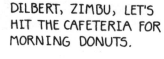

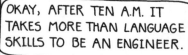

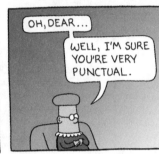

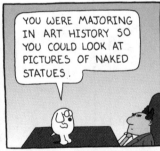

ENGINEERS

Row 1

MY PATENT APPLICATION IS COMPLETE. SOON THE OTHER ENGINEERS WILL COME SNIFFING AROUND.

THEY ARE ATTRACTED BY THE SCENT OF SUCCESS. THEY WANT THEIR NAMES ON MY PATENT.

THE SCENT CAN'T BE COMING FROM HERE.

WE MAY BE GETTING A FALSE POSITIVE FROM HIS BALONEY SANDWICH.

Row 2

THE LOCAL SCHOOL WANTS SOMEBODY TO TALK TO THE KIDS ABOUT A CAREER AS AN ENGINEER.

I'M GIVING THIS PLUM ASSIGNMENT TO YOU BECAUSE YOU'RE SUCH A GOOD ROLE MODEL.

HEE HEE

IT'S MORE SINCERE SOUNDING WHEN YOU DON'T GIGGLE.

REMEMBER, CHILDREN ARE OUR FUTURE!

Row 3

DILBERT TALKS TO A CLASS ABOUT CAREER OPTIONS.

AND DON'T FORGET THE SOCIAL LIFE THAT COMES WITH BEING AN ENGINEER.

NINETY PERCENT OF ALL ENGINEERS ARE GUYS, SO IT'S A BONANZA OF DATING OPPORTUNITIES FOR THE LADIES WHO ENTER THE FIELD.

FOR THE MEN, THERE ARE THESE LITTLE VIDEO GAME DEVICES...

BEEP BEEP

WOULD I BE ALLOWED TO DATE A NON-ENGINEER?

Row 4

DILBERT TALKS TO A CLASS ABOUT CAREER OPTIONS.

THE GOAL OF EVERY ENGINEER IS TO RETIRE WITHOUT GETTING BLAMED FOR A MAJOR CATASTROPHE.

ENGINEERS PREFER TO WORK AS "CONSULTANTS" ON PROJECT TEAMS. THAT WAY THERE'S NO REAL WORK, BLAME IS SPREAD ACROSS THE GROUP, AND YOU CAN CRUSH ANY IDEA FROM MARKETING!

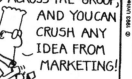

...AND SOMETIMES YOU GET FREE DONUTS JUST FOR SHOWING UP!

GET OUT OF MY CLASS-ROOM.

ENGINEERS

Panel 1: I JUST READ THAT A NEW COMPUTER CHIP IS ON THE MARKET. YOUR MACHINE IS OUT OF DATE.

Panel 2: YOU'RE BEHIND THE CURVE. TECHNOLOGY IS RACING AHEAD WITHOUT YOU. YOU'RE NO LONGER STATE-OF-THE-ART OR LEADING EDGE.

Panel 3: SOMETIMES PEOPLE LIKE YOU CAN GET JOBS IN MUSEUMS. I BOUGHT THIS THING YESTERDAY!!

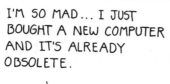

Panel 4: I'M SO MAD... I JUST BOUGHT A NEW COMPUTER AND IT'S ALREADY OBSOLETE.

Panel 5: DON'T FEEL BAD. THE OTHER ENGINEERS WON'T LOOK DOWN ON YOU JUST BECAUSE YOU'RE BEHIND THE TECHNOLOGY CURVE.

Panel 6: YEAH, WE WILL. NOT RIGHT IN FRONT OF HIM.

Panel 7: I HATE MY SHIRTS. EACH ONE HAS EITHER A STAIN OR A MISSING BUTTON.

Panel 8: THEY SAY ENGINEERS ARE NOT CONCERNED WITH FASHION, BUT THAT'S NOT FAIR.

Panel 9: WHICH STAIN GOES WITH THIS TIE? DEFINITELY THE MARINARA.

Panel 10: THIS WEEK I DISCOVERED THAT THE DEMAND FOR ENGINEERS EXCEEDS THE SUPPLY.

Panel 11: I RESPONDED BY INCREASING MY INSOLENCE AND DECREASING MY PRODUCTIVITY.

Panel 12: I WILL NEVER HIRE ANOTHER ENGINEER AS LONG AS I'M ALIVE. EQUILIBRIUM HAS BEEN RESTORED.

HERE'S SOME NICE CHOCOLATE CAKE FOR YOU AND DOGBERT.

THANKS, MOM.

THANKS, MOM.

TELL ME ALL ABOUT YOUR JOB AT THE RAILROAD.

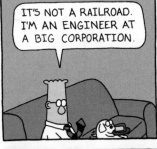

IT'S NOT A RAILROAD. I'M AN ENGINEER AT A BIG CORPORATION.

DO YOU FIX THE TYPEWRITERS WHEN THEY BREAK?

NO... TODAY I DEBUGGED A TCP/IP DRIVER FOR AN APPLICATION THAT RUNS OVER ISDN WITH BONDING.

YOU MEAN, ALL YOU DO IS SLAP A BRI ANALYZER ON A CIRCUIT AND LOOK FOR BAD PACKETS?

WELL... YEAH.

BUT IT'S REALLY HARD.

I WAS DOING OKAY UNTIL SHE OFFERED TO PAY MY TUITION TO TYPEWRITER REPAIR SCHOOL.

YOU SHOULDN'T HAVE COMPARED HER CAKE TO PACKING FOAM.

LET ME INTRODUCE YOU TO ONE OF OUR ENGINEERS.

KAREN IS OUR NEW VICE PRESIDENT. AND YOU ARE...?

DILBERT: VALUED EMPLOYEE.

I BELIEVE IN OPEN COMMUNICATIONS, DILBERT. FEEL FREE TO TALK ABOUT ANYTHING.

UH-OH

SO, WHAT WERE YOU WORKING ON?

OH-NO

WELL... I WAS JUST SENDING AN E-MAIL TO SOMEBODY WHO SITS BY A WINDOW TO ASK IF IT'S RAINING.

IF IT'S RAINING I'LL FASHION A RAINCOAT FROM A LARGE TRASH BAG.

WATCH.

THREE HOLES AND YOU'RE READY TO GO!

ARE YOU PLANNING TO GO OUT AT LUNCH?

ONLY IF IT RAINS.

IF THIS COMPANY WON'T USE OUR PRODUCT IDEA LET'S QUIT AND START OUR OWN BUSINESS!

WHY QUIT? WE CAN RUN OUR NEW COMPANY FROM OUR CUBICLES AND GET PAID TOO.

WOULDN'T THAT BE IMMORAL?

THAT'S ONLY AN ISSUE FOR PEOPLE WHO AREN'T ALREADY IN HELL.

IT HAS COME TO MY ATTENTION THAT SOME EMPLOYEES ARE RUNNING SIDE BUSINESSES FROM THEIR CUBICLES.

REALLY??

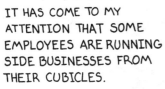

I DON'T WANT TO SEE ANY SIGNS OF THAT IN MY DEPARTMENT.

FAIR ENOUGH.

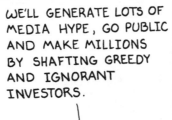

SOFTWARE OUTLET

SALE

PALMS READ $25

SHOE WORLD

WHAT ABOUT "YELLOW PAGES" ADS?

WALBERT INC.

THE BUSINESS PLAN FOR YOUR START-UP IS IDIOTIC BUT I'M GOING TO PROVIDE THE VENTURE CAPITAL FUNDING ANYWAY.

WE'LL GENERATE LOTS OF MEDIA HYPE, GO PUBLIC AND MAKE MILLIONS BY SHAFTING GREEDY AND IGNORANT INVESTORS.
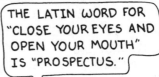

THE LATIN WORD FOR "CLOSE YOUR EYES AND OPEN YOUR MOUTH" IS "PROSPECTUS."

THIS IS EXACTLY WHY I'M AFRAID OF DOGS.

WALLY AND I STARTED OUR OWN COMPANY. WE'RE SELLING THE PRODUCT THAT YOU SAID NOBODY WANTS.

SOON WE WILL BE RICH.
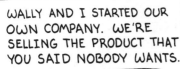

WE DO OUR VICTORY JIG IN YOUR FACE.

BA-BUM

WHEN HE SHOWED YOU YOUR EMPLOYMENT AGREEMENT — WHERE YOU GAVE ALL PATENT RIGHTS TO THIS COMPANY — WHAT PART OF THE JIG WERE YOU DOING?

TURBO MOONING.

SOB

ENTREPRENEURS AND VENTURE CAPITALISTS

ENTREPRENEURS AND VENTURE CAPITALISTS

VENTURE CAPITALISTS

DESPITE YOUR COOL PONYTAIL, YOU SEEM TO HAVE SQUANDERED OUR INVESTMENT.

YOU'LL GET NO MORE FUNDING UNLESS YOU MUTTER EMPTY INTERNET WORDS THAT MAKE US SWOON!

E-COMMERCE.

GURGLE

HOW'S YOUR INTERNET START-UP COMPANY COMING?

GOOD.

MY PLAN IS TO BE THE DOMINANT INTERNET SOURCE FOR TUNA SANDWICHES.

SO, IF I BUY ONE, YOU SHIP IT OVER-NIGHT?

NO, YOU HAVE TO COME PICK IT UP.

I'M STARTING MY OWN VENTURE CAPITAL FIRM.

I'M ATTRACTED TO THE CONCEPT OF WATCHING PEOPLE WITH MORONIC IDEAS BEG FOR MONEY.

WILL YOU ACTUALLY FINANCE ANYBODY?

THAT WOULD SORT OF CRIMP THE MIRTH.

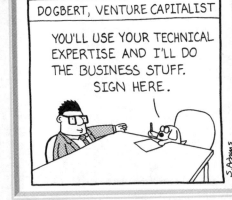

DOGBERT, VENTURE CAPITALIST

YOU'LL USE YOUR TECHNICAL EXPERTISE AND I'LL DO THE BUSINESS STUFF. SIGN HERE.

SINCE YOU'RE THE INVENTOR OF THE TECH-NOLOGY, YOU'LL GET 100% OF THE SPECIAL DECORATIVE NON-EQUITY STOCK. I'LL SETTLE FOR ALL THE COMMON STOCK.

I HOPE WE CAN AVOID THE TENSION THAT SOME PARTNERS EXPERI-ENCE.

GIVE ME MY PEN, YOU MISCREANT.

DOGBERT, VENTURE CAPITALIST

MY IDEA IS TO DEVELOP A WORD PROCESSING PROGRAM FOR WINDOWS.

THAT'S AN INTERESTING CONCEPT. I WONDER IF TWENTY DOLLARS WOULD BE ENOUGH.

TO START A SOFTWARE COMPANY?

NO, TO PAY OUR WAITRESS TO BEAT YOU WITH A LOAF OF FRENCH BREAD.

DOGBERT, VENTURE CAPITALIST

I'LL INVEST UP TO FIVE MILLION DOLLARS IF YOU'LL AGREE TO SOME STANDARD CONDITIONS.

I WILL BE CHAIRMAN OF THE BOARD AND OWN 99% OF THE COMPANY. YOU WILL WORK FOR FREE AND WASH MY CAR TWICE A WEEK.

CAN I MOW YOUR LAWN INSTEAD OF WASHING YOUR CAR?

YOU'RE A TOUGH BARGAINER, BUT I PREFER MULTIMEDIA DEVELOPERS FOR MY GARDENING NEEDS.

HI! I WANT TO BE YOUR FINANCIAL ADVISOR.

I'VE COME TO LIVE WITH YOU. WE'LL EVENTUALLY FORM A LIFELONG BOND OF TRUST AND FRIENDSHIP.

I LIKED IT BETTER WHEN YOU GUYS JUST TOOK OUR MONEY.

I RECOMMEND A STRATEGY CALLED "CHURN."

I RECOMMEND OUR "CHURN 'N' BURN" FAMILY OF MUTUAL FUNDS.

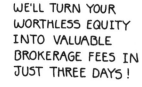

WE'LL TURN YOUR WORTHLESS EQUITY INTO VALUABLE BROKERAGE FEES IN JUST THREE DAYS!

IS IT RISKY?

ARE YOU KIDDING?! WE HAVE ACTUAL BROCHURES!

Panel 1:

FOR THE TIMID INVESTOR, I RECOMMEND OUR "PERPETUAL CERTIFICATES OF DEPOSIT."

Panel 2:

THEY EARN THE HIGHEST POSSIBLE INTEREST. THE ONLY TRADE-OFF IS THAT YOU CAN NEVER WITHDRAW IT.

Panel 3:

WHY DON'T I JUST FLING MY MONEY OUT A WINDOW?

AH, YOU'VE HEARD OF OUR "FLYING DEBENTURE" PRODUCT?

Panel 4:

I'M GOING INTO BUSINESS AS A FINANCIAL ADVISOR.

SOUNDS HARD.

Panel 5:

IT'S EASY. I'LL TELL ALL MY CLIENTS TO INVEST IN THE "DOGBERT DEFERRED EARNINGS FUND."

Panel 6:

ISN'T THAT A CONFLICT OF INTEREST?

ONLY IF I SHOW INTEREST IN THE CLIENT.

Panel 7:

DOGBERT: FINANCIAL ADVISOR

STOCKS... ANNUITIES... DERIVATIVES... CAPITAL GAINS TAX...

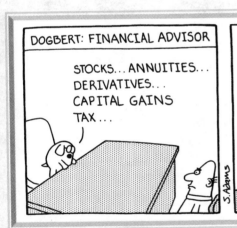

Panel 8:

IT'S ALL TOO CONFUSING FOR YOU!! GIVE ME ALL YOUR MONEY NOW OR YOU'LL DIE A PAUPER!! NOW! NOW! BEFORE INTEREST RATES FALL!!

Panel 9:

WILL THIS REDUCE MY INCOME TAXES?

MORE THAN YOU MIGHT GUESS.

Panel 10:

DOGBERT: FINANCIAL ADVISOR

HERE'S A PICTURE OF YOU LIVING IN A DUMPSTER IN TWENTY YEARS.

Panel 11:

BUT IF YOU INVEST IN THE "DOGBERT DEFERRED INCOME FUND" TAKE A LOOK AT WHAT YOU COULD OWN SOMEDAY!!

Panel 12:

I COULD OWN A MANSION?!!

YOU COULD OWN A PHOTOGRAPH.

THAT'S OUR NEW "STRATEGIC DIVERSIFICATION FUND."

OUR LAWYERS PUT YOUR MONEY IN LITTLE BAGS, THEN WE HAVE TRAINED DOGS BURY THEM AROUND TOWN.

DO THEY BURY THE BAGS OR THE LAWYERS?

WE'VE TRIED IT BOTH WAYS.

I HIRED A NEW DIRECTOR OF HUMAN RESOURCES TO HANDLE THE DOWNSIZING.

I NEEDED SOMEBODY WHO ACTS LIKE A FRIEND BUT SECRETLY DELIGHTS IN THE MISERY OF ALL PEOPLE.

WE NEED TO TALK, PAUL. BUT FIRST I'M GOING TO BAT YOUR HEAD AROUND AND SCRATCH YOU.

HEE HEE!! THAT'S SO CUTE!

CATBERT: EVIL H.R. DIRECTOR

MY BOSS IS PREVENTING ME FROM TRANSFERING TO A GREAT JOB.

THAT'S OUTRAGEOUS! THERE SHOULDN'T BE ANY GREAT JOBS IN THIS COMPANY.

ONCE AGAIN, YOU'VE MADE A BAD SITUATION WORSE.

THAT'S THE HUMAN RESOURCES PROMISE.

CATBERT: EVIL H.R. DIRECTOR

THE COMPANY KNOWS EVERYTHING ABOUT YOU, WALLY.

WE HAVE LOGS OF ALL YOUR PHONE CALLS, WEB HITS AND E-MAIL. WE HAVE YOUR URINE TEST, COLLEGE GRADES, SALARY AND FAMILY CONTACTS...

IT'S AGAINST OUR POLICY TO KILL EMPLOYEES AND REPLACE THEM WITH LOW-PAID IMPERSONATORS, BUT I WANTED YOU TO KNOW IT'S FEASIBLE.

CATBERT: EVIL H.R. DIRECTOR

YOU LOOK STRESSED OUT, ALICE.

I COULD FIX THAT BY BECOMING A CHAMPION FOR IMPROVEMENTS IN THE WORKPLACE.

OR I COULD GIVE YOU A LITTLE BOOKLET CALLED "STRESS NO MORE."

HMM... I WONDER WHICH WAY IS BEST.

"STRESS IS YOUR BODY'S WAY OF SAYING..."

"...YOU HAVEN'T WORKED ENOUGH UNPAID OVERTIME."

I'VE NEVER SEEN A WOMAN'S FOREHEAD IGNITE HER HAIR BEFORE.

MISTER CATBERT WILL EXPLAIN OUR NEW "TOTAL COMPENSATION PLAN" FOR EXCELLENCE.

WE NO LONGER VIEW COMPENSATION IN THE NARROW TERMS OF SALARY ALONE.

DANGER! DANGER!

IF EMPLOYEE BENEFITS GO UP, THEN SALARIES CAN GO DOWN AND IT ALL BALANCES OUT.

FOR EXAMPLE, DID YOU KNOW YOU COULD LOWER YOUR BLOOD PRESSURE BY RUBBING MY SOFT, FURRY BELLY?

IT MIGHT BE A TRICK!

WHAT'S THE WORST THING THAT COULD HAPPEN?

HA HA HA!!! IT'S A HEALTH BENEFIT! NOW I'LL CUT EVERYBODY'S SALARY!

I'VE NOTICED THAT THE MORE HEALTH BENEFITS I GET, THE WORSE I FEEL.

CATBERT: EVIL H.R. DIRECTOR

I'M HAVING TROUBLE FINDING QUALIFIED EXTERNAL APPLICANTS.

ALL I HAVE ARE A HEADLESS MAN, A MIME, AND A FROZEN CRO-MAGNON GUY WE FOUND IN A GLACIER.

DOES THE MIME BRING HIS OWN INVISIBLE CUBICLE? I LOVE THOSE!

ONLY IF WE PAY HIS RELOCATION COSTS.

CATBERT: EVIL H.R. DIRECTOR

ALICE, THE EXPERTS SAY YOU NEED TO BALANCE WORK AND HOME LIFE.

YOU WORKED 80 HOURS LAST WEEK. THAT'S LESS THAN HALF OF THE HOURS IN A WEEK.

GIVE US SOME BALANCE, YOU SELFISH HAG.

THIS CONVERSATION TOOK A NASTY TURN.

CATBERT: EVIL H.R. DIRECTOR

ARE YOU ABLE TO WORK WHILE BEING CONSTANTLY INTERRUPTED?

NO. I WOULD BE TOTALLY INEFFECTIVE, JUST LIKE ANYONE ELSE.

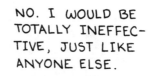

WE WERE DONE WITH THE SECTION YOU HAD TO ANSWER HONESTLY.

OH. IN THAT CASE, INTERRUPTIONS MAKE ME STRONGER.

CATBERT: EVIL H.R. DIRECTOR

YOUR PERSONAL LIVES REFLECT ON THIS COMPANY.

FROM NOW ON, A STRICT DRESS CODE WILL BE ENFORCED IN YOUR HOMES.

ON THE PLUS SIDE, IT'S ONE LESS DECISION I HAVE TO MAKE EVERY DAY.

CATBERT THE H.R. DIRECTOR

ASOK, IT'S TIME TO GROOM YOU FOR MANAGEMENT.

I DON'T SEE TOO MANY BUGS IN YOUR FUR.

CAN YOU LICK THE TOP OF YOUR OWN HEAD?

NO, I CAN'T.

THEN YOU CAN'T BE A MANAGER.

CATBERT THE HR DIRECTOR

I THINK I'LL INVENT SOME ILLOGICAL POLICIES TO ANNOY EMPLOYEES.

MY DIABOLICAL NEW DRESS CODE WILL MAKE THEM QUESTION THEIR OWN SANITY.

...SO, CASUAL CLOTHES DON'T LOWER OUR STOCK VALUE... BUT ONLY IF WORN ON FRIDAYS... UNLESS SOMEBODY SEES US... GOT IT?

I THINK I'M INSANE.

AS DIRECTOR OF HUMAN RESOURCES I HAVE DEVELOPED A POLICY FOR HANDLING THE EMPLOYEES WHO COMPLAIN.

IT'S A BIG HOLE. I'LL TRICK THE WHINERS INTO GETTING IN IT. AND THEN I'LL COVER THEM WITH SAND.

I DON'T SEE HOW THIS COULD POSSIBLY WORK.

THERE'S A DETAILED EXPLANATION AT THE BOTTOM OF THE HOLE.

CATBERT THE H.R. DIRECTOR

MY JOB IS TOO STRESSFUL. CAN I SEE A COMPANY COUNSELOR?

I RE-ENGINEERED OUR COUNSELING PROCESS. NOW WE PUT YOU IN A BIG HOLE AND COVER YOU WITH SAND.

IF THIS IS MY ONLY BENEFIT I'D BETTER GET A LOT OF SAND!

JUST KEEP YOUR MOUTH OPEN.

HUMAN RESOURCES

GUESS WHAT, WALLY.

WHAT SADISTIC PLOT HAS H.R. COME UP WITH NOW, CATBERT?

WE'RE GIVING YOU A REAL BOSS PLUS A "DOTTED LINE" TO ANOTHER BOSS WHO HAS DIFFERENT OBJECTIVES.

THE STATUS REPORTS ALONE WILL TAKE FORTY HOURS A WEEK.

I'M GONNA STAPLE MYSELF TO DEATH.

© 1995 United Feature Syndicate, Inc.(NYC)

CATBERT, H.R. DIRECTOR

I'VE COME TO GIVE YOU "EMPLOYEE ORIENTATION," WALLY.

BUT I'VE WORKED HERE FOR YEARS.

YOU STILL HAVE A GLIMMER OF HOPE. YOU'LL HAVE TO WATCH THIS MANDATORY TRAINING VIDEO.

HOPE

SO, YOU STILL HAVE HOPE...

RELAX... LET IT GO.

4/29/96 © 1996 United Feature Syndicate, Inc.(NYC)

CATBERT: EVIL H.R. DIRECTOR

THERE'S BEEN A SLIGHT CHANGE IN THE VACATION POLICY.

ARE WE GETTING MORE VACATION DAYS?

YOU MUST BE NEW HERE.

AS YOU KNOW, ALL VACATION TIME MUST BE USED IN THE YEAR IT IS EARNED.

I REALIZE THIS IS NOT ALWAYS CONVENIENT. SO I'VE DECIDED TO BE FLEXIBLE.

© 1998 United Feature Syndicate, Inc.

3/22/98

FROM NOW ON, ANY TIME YOU SPEND IN THE RESTROOM WILL COUNT AS VACATION.

WE SHOULD COMPLAIN.

IF YOU NEED ME, I'LL BE TAKING A PORCELAIN CRUISE.

CATBERT: EVIL HR DIRECTOR

IT HAS COME TO MY ATTENTION THAT YOU USED COMPANY RESOURCES TO SEND E-MAIL TO YOUR BOYFRIEND

I'M WILLING TO OVER-LOOK THIS UGLY INCIDENT IN EXCHANGE FOR FIVE MINUTES OF QUALITY PETTING ON MY SOFT, FURRY BELLY.

THIS SEEMS SO WRONG.

TRY USING BOTH HANDS.

COMPANY HEADQUARTERS

DOES ANYBODY HAVE A PLAN FOR GETTING RID OF THE EMPLOYEES?

WELL, THEY'RE BAD AT MATH; WE COULD OFFER DECEPTIVELY SMALL SUMS OF MONEY TO PEOPLE WHO RETIRE.

HEY, THIS COULD BE GOOD.

IT'S BEEN A LONG TIME SINCE I HAD TO CALCULATE THE COSINE OF ANYTHING.

CATBERT: EVIL H.R. DIRECTOR

YOU'VE BEEN A GOOD CONTRACT EMPLOYEE. WE'D LIKE TO MAKE YOU A REGULAR EMPLOYEE.

YOU MEAN YOU WANT TO PAY ME LESS?

WE WANT YOU TO BE MOTIVATED BY SOME-THING OTHER THAN MONEY.

LIKE... STUPIDITY?

CATBERT: EVIL H.R. DIRECTOR

I'M GROSSLY UNDER-PAID FOR THE TYPE OF WORK I DO NOW.

WRITE A DESCRIPTION OF YOUR CURRENT DUTIES. I'LL BE HAPPY TO DO A COMPENSATION REVIEW.

BASED ON A TRUE STORY

SADLY, IT APPEARS YOU'RE NOT QUALIFIED FOR YOUR OWN JOB. BUT ONE OF YOUR SUBORDINATES IS.

CATBERT: EVIL H.R. DIRECTOR
MY EYES ARE SORE FROM USING THE COMPUTER.

TRY TYPING WITH YOUR FINGERS, THE WAY EVERYONE ELSE DOES.

PERSONALLY, I FIND COMPUTERS VERY RESTFUL ON MY EYES.

CATBERT: H.R. DIRECTOR
WHEN YOU DUMPED MORE WORK ON WALLY, DID HE MOAN? OR DID HE SCREAM?

IT SOUNDED LIKE THIS ... AAOO-MUW AAHH-OW-OW!!

THE STAFFING LEVELS SOUND ABOUT RIGHT.

CATBERT: EVIL H.R. DIRECTOR
I'M NOT ENJOYING MY JOB.

TAKE THIS POWERFUL ANTI-DEPRESSANT DRUG FOR THE REST OF YOUR LIFE.
I DIDN'T KNOW H.R. COULD PRESCRIBE DRUGS.

I'D HATE TO LIVE IN A WORLD WHERE THAT WAS ILLEGAL.
"BOSS-PROOF CAP."

CATBERT: EVIL H.R. DIRECTOR
THE COMPANY'S GOAL IS TO DOUBLE THE EFFICIENCY OF ALL EMPLOYEES.

QUESTION: IF WE DOUBLE OUR EFFICIENCY, WON'T YOU DOWNSIZE HALF OF US?

DON'T TALK TO ANYONE IN MARKETING; THEY AREN'T SO GOOD AT MATH.

AS DIRECTOR OF HUMAN RESOURCES I'VE BEEN ASKED TO REDUCE THE COST OF EMPLOYEE BENEFITS.

THE COMPANY WILL NO LONGER PAY FOR EYE-GLASSES. BUT WE WILL SUPPORT A NEW VISION-CORRECTION PROCEDURE.

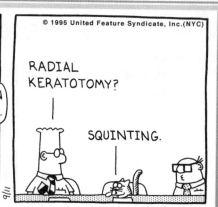

© 1995 United Feature Syndicate, Inc.(NYC)

RADIAL KERATOTOMY?

SQUINTING.

CATBERT, THE EVIL DIRECTOR OF HUMAN RESOURCES

ACCORDING TO MY SOURCES, YOU'VE BEEN ENJOYING YOUR JOB, WALLY.

IT WAS TEMPORARY. I DON'T KNOW WHAT GOT INTO ME...

PLEASE REFER TO PAGE ONE OF THE EMPLOYEE MANUAL.

"JOB SATISFACTION IS THE SAME AS STEALING FROM THE COMPANY." I'LL HAVE TO CHARGE YOU FOR ADMISSION UNLESS I START HEARING SOME SHRIEKS OF PAIN.

CATBERT, THE EVIL DIRECTOR OF HUMAN RESOURCES

WE'RE MOVING TO "CAFETERIA STYLE" BENEFITS.

UNDER THIS SYSTEM, IF YOU NEED HEALTH CARE, YOU WANDER THROUGH THE CAFETERIA ASKING "DOES ANYBODY KNOW WHAT THIS RED LUMP IS?"

WHAT IF IT'S A LIFE-THREATENING PROBLEM?

THAT REMINDS ME, THE CAFETERIA WON'T BE LABELING THE ENTREES ANYMORE.

CATBERT, H.R. DIRECTOR

WALLY, IT MIGHT NOT SEEM FAIR THAT NEW EMPLOYEES ARE PAID MORE THAN YOU...

BUT YOU COULD ALWAYS QUIT AND THEN REAPPLY FOR YOUR OLD JOB AT A HIGHER SALARY.

I JUST MIGHT DO THAT!!

WOULD YOU MIND RUBBING THIS CATNIP ALL OVER YOUR BODY FIRST?

CATBERT THE H.R. DIRECTOR

THIS REPORT SAYS YOU WENT NUTS AT A VENDING MACHINE BECAUSE IT TOOK YOUR MONEY.

THE COMPANY USED TO OFFER COUNSELING IN THESE CASES. BUT WE FOUND IT WAS MORE ECONOMICAL TO APPLY THE DEATH PENALTY.

WHAT?! HOW IS THAT POSSIBLE?

I'M NOT SURE YET. YOU'RE TOO BIG FOR THE MICRO-WAVE OVEN...

CATBERT THE EVIL HUMAN RESOURCES DIRECTOR

THE EMPLOYEES HAVE TOO MUCH TIME OFF. IT MUST BE STOPPED.

I SUMMON THE DEMONS OF DARKNESS TO ASSIST ME!!!

...ELIMINATE SICK DAYS. MAKE THEM USE VACATION DAYS WHEN THEY'RE ILL. CALL IT A "TIME BANK."

IT'S PLAYFUL... IT'S CRUEL... I LIKE IT.

I AM MORDAC, THE PREVENTER OF INFOR-MATION SERVICES. I BRING NEW GUIDELINES FOR PASSWORDS.

"ALL PASSWORDS MUST BE AT LEAST SIX CHARACTERS LONG... INCLUDE NUMBERS AND LETTERS... INCLUDE A MIX OF UPPER AND LOWER CASE..."

"USE DIFFERENT PASS-WORDS FOR EACH SYSTEM. CHANGE ONCE A MONTH. DO NOT WRITE ANY-THING DOWN."

SQUEAL LIKE A PIG!!!

I AM MORDAC, THE PREVENTER OF INFOR-MATION SERVICES. I COME TO CONFISCATE YOUR NON-STANDARD COMPUTER.

YOU'LL GIVE ME A NEW ONE, RIGHT?

THIS IS HEAVIER THAN IT LOOKS.

I'LL HAVE TO DISABLE IT AND LEAVE IT HERE.

THE NEW ONE IS ALREADY ON ITS WAY, RIGHT?

INFORMATION SERVICES

I AM MORDAC, THE PREVENTER OF INFORMATION SERVICES!

I'LL TAKE YOUR COMPUTER AND YOUR LITTLE P.D.A. TOO!

DO YOU RECOGNIZE THIS?

AAAGH! THAT'S MY NETWORK CABLE!

WHAT DO YOU WANT FROM ME?!

MORDAC, IT IS I, CATBERT, THE EVIL DIRECTOR OF HUMAN RESOURCES!

YOU MADE MY PERSONAL PRINTER A SHARED DEVICE!

GRRRR!! AAAGH!!

TWO WRONGS MADE A RIGHT.

WELCOME TO MY REALITY.

WHY DID THE I.S. DEPARTMENT DENY MY REQUEST FOR A PC UPGRADE?

BECAUSE WE ARE EVIL INCARNATE!! BUWAHAHAHA!!

I WAS LOOKING FOR SOMETHING MORE SPECIFIC.

YOU DIDN'T PROVIDE A DOLLAR ESTIMATE OF THE BENEFITS.

THAT'S RIDICULOUS. I CAN'T PUT A VALUE ON EVERY TOOL I NEED TO DO MY JOB.

IF YOU CAN'T QUANTIFY IT, THEN IT MUST NOT BE NECESSARY.

THEN WHY DOES THE COMPANY GIVE ME A CHAIR? I CAN'T QUANTIFY THAT EITHER?

HERE'S ONE MORE REASON WHY IT STINKS TO BE ME.

Panel 1: REQUEST DENIED. THE INFORMATION SERVICES DEPARTMENT DOES NOT UPGRADE NON-STANDARD COMPUTERS.

Panel 2: IT'S NOT AN UPGRADE. IT'S A REPLACEMENT.

OUR POLICY IS THAT IT'S AN UPGRADE UNLESS YOU DISCARD THE OLD ONE.

Panel 3: YOUR TRASH IS DECLINED. OUR POLICY IS "NO COMPUTERS."

© 1998 United Feature Syndicate, Inc.

Panel 1: I'M NOT ALLOWED TO GET A NEW COMPUTER UNTIL I GET RID OF THIS OLD ONE.

Panel 2: THE JANITOR WON'T ALLOW IT IN THE TRASH; UNION RULES WON'T LET ME CARRY IT TO STORAGE. SO I BUILT THIS CATAPULT.

Panel 3: LIKE I ALWAYS SAY, EVERY PROBLEM HAS AN ENGINEERING SOLUTION.

© 1998 United Feature Syndicate, Inc.

Panel 1: I AM MORDAC THE REFUSER. I AM HERE TO DISCUSS YOUR REQUEST FOR A COMPUTER UPGRADE.

Panel 2: CRINKLE! MMPHH! CHOMP CHOMP CHOMP

Panel 3: WE LOTHT THUH PAHPER-WUHK.

THAT'S A HUGE SURPRISE. LUCKILY I MADE SEVENTY-FIVE EXTRA COPIES.

© 1997 United Feature Syndicate, Inc.

Panel 1: I AM MORDAC THE PREVENTER, YOUR LIASON FROM THE INFORMATION TECHNOLOGY DEPARTMENT.

Panel 2: I COME WITH TALES OF RESOURCE SHORTAGES. YOUR REQUEST FOR OUR SERVICES IS DENIED.

Panel 3: I DIDN'T REQUEST ANY OF YOUR SERVICES.

DON'T TRY YOUR REVERSE PSYCHOLOGY ON ME.

© 1997 United Feature Syndicate, Inc.

HEY, EVERYBODY. MEET OUR NEW INTERN, ASOK.

I HOPE THIS ONE'S STURDIER THAN THE LAST ONE.

MY STAPLE REMOVER IS BROKEN. SOMEBODY TOSS THAT INTERN TO ME!

ASOK THE INTERN

AS AN INTERN, YOUR ASSIGNMENTS WON'T BE AS GLAMOROUS AS MINE, BUT YOU'LL GAIN EXPERIENCE.

DILBERT, I NEED A STATUS REPORT ON THE MOUSE PAD INVENTORY.

SEE? MY ASSIGNMENT HAS THE WORD "STATUS" BUILT RIGHT IN.

DANGER! ALERT!

ASOK THE INTERN

ASOK, COME QUICKLY! IT'S AN EMERGENCY!

YOU MUST CRAWL THROUGH THE JEFFRIES TUBE AND SHUT DOWN THE FURNACE BEFORE IT FRIES US ALL!

TODAY YOUNG ASOK LEARNS THAT LIFE IS NOT LIKE "STAR TREK."

I'M STUCK.

SPANK THE INTERN 50¢

ASOK THE INTERN

I CAME IN OVER THE WEEKEND AND LOOKED AT THE DESIGN YOU'VE BEEN WORKING WITH ALL YEAR.

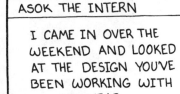

IT TURNS OUT THAT YOU COULD HAVE BUILT THE UNIT AT HALF THE COST WITH JUST ONE MINOR CHANGE.

IS IT TRUE I CAN WIN AWARDS FOR THIS SORT OF THING?

FETCH THE INTERNAPULT.

INTERNS AND CO-OPS

I AM ONLY A LOWLY INTERN, BUT I SEE AN OBVIOUS SOLUTION TO YOUR PROBLEM.

JUST CLICK HERE... CLEAR YOUR BUFFERS AND INITIALIZE THE LINK... NOW USE THIS CODE PATCH FOR THE MEMORY LEAK.

THIS IS FUNNY IF YOU CONSIDER THAT YOUR SALARY IS TWICE AS MUCH AS MINE.

I'M LAUGHING ON THE INSIDE.

© 1996 United Feature Syndicate, Inc.

MY NEW PRODUCT IS A DATABASE OF FAMOUS SERIAL KILLERS.

YOU CAN SEARCH THE DATABASE BY NAME, WEAPON OR TATTOO.

LET ME GUESS, WALLY: SIX MONTHS AGO OUR YOUNG INTERN ASKED YOU WHAT THE TERM "KILLER APPLICATION" MEANT.

© 1998 United Feature Syndicate, Inc.

AS A CO-OP EMPLOYEE, YOU CAN'T EXPECT THE SAME LUSH CUBICLE ENVIRONMENT THAT THE REGULAR EMPLOYEES ENJOY.

YOU'LL BE SHARING THIS CUBICLE WITH OUR OTHER CO-OPS.

I HEARD THAT THE NEW CO-OP ONLY LASTED ONE DAY.

HE DIDN'T FIT IN.

© 1996 United Feature Syndicate, Inc. (NYC)

WE'LL BE HAVING AN ISO 9000 AUDIT SOON. THEY'LL CHECK TO SEE IF WE FOLLOW OUR OWN DOCUMENTED PROCEDURES FOR EVERYTHING WE DO.

I'VE DIVIDED OUR PREPARATION TASKS INTO TWO GROUPS: UNETHICAL AND UNPRODUCTIVE.

I'LL TRAIN OUR DEPARTMENT TO LIE TO THE AUDITOR. YOU CAN DOCUMENT OUR INANE PROCEDURES.

NO FAIR. YOU DID UNETHICAL LAST TIME TOO!

© 1996 United Feature Syndicate, Inc. (NYC)

CAROL, I NEED TO DOCUMENT YOUR PROCEDURE FOR ORDERING OFFICE SUPPLIES. IT'S AN ISO 9000 REQUIREMENT.

IF SOMEONE ASKS FOR SOMETHING, I CHECK THE SUPPLY CABINET FIRST. THEN I SAY, "THERE'S ONE LEFT. YOU CAN'T HAVE IT BECAUSE THEN WE'D BE ALL OUT."

THEN I SPEND THE REST OF THE DAY COMPLAINING ABOUT THE PERSON WHO ASKED.

UH-OH... I'M OUT OF INK.

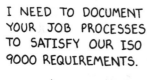

I NEED TO DOCUMENT YOUR JOB PROCESSES TO SATISFY OUR ISO 9000 REQUIREMENTS.

OKAY.

I TRY TO ANTICIPATE THE SHIFTING POLITICAL WINDS. THEN I WRAP MYSELF IN THE RELEVANT BUZZWORDS AND TRY TO ACHIEVE IMPORTANCE WITHOUT ADDING VALUE.

WHAT'S YOUR JOB TITLE?

DIRECTOR OF ISO 9000 QUALITY PROCESS DESIGN.

YOUR PRODUCT LOOKS GOOD, BUT YOU CAN'T BE OUR SUPPLIER UNLESS YOUR COMPANY IS ISO 9000 CERTIFIED.

SO... YOU DON'T CARE HOW BAD OUR INTERNAL PROCESSES ARE, AS LONG AS THEY'RE WELL-DOCUMENTED AND USED CONSISTENTLY?

THAT'S RIGHT.

OUR DOCUMENTED PROCESS SAYS I MUST NOW LAUGH IN YOUR FACE AND DOUBLE OUR PRICE.

WE'RE HAVING AN ISO 9000 AUDIT THIS WEEK.

TAKE A LOOK AT YOUR DOCUMENTED JOB DESCRIPTIONS AND MAKE SURE THAT IT'S WHAT YOU'RE DOING IF THE AUDITOR ASKS.

ACCORDING TO THIS I'M SOME SORT OF ENGINEER.

AS IF WE'D HAVE TIME FOR THAT...

DILBERT *Gives You the Business*

WHY ARE YOU PUTTING A SIGN ON THE COFFEE MAKER?

IT'S AN ISO 9000 REQUIREMENT. EVERYTHING MUST BE CLEARLY LABELED. THERE CAN BE NO EXCEPTIONS.

THAT'S STUPID.

BELIEVE ME, I DON'T LIKE IT ANY MORE THAN YOU DO.

STUPID LABEL GUY

I'M PUTTING YOU IN CHARGE OF GETTING OUR "ISO 9000" CERTIFICATION.

WE DON'T KNOW WHAT IT IS, BUT IT LOOKS GREAT ON BROCHURES.

I THINK IT CERTIFIES THAT WE FOLLOW A CONSISTENT PROCESS.

THAT'S US; WE ALWAYS LIE ON OUR BROCHURES.

THANK YOU FOR COMING TO THE "ISO 9000" PROJECT KICK-OFF MEETING.

EACH OF YOU WAS HAND-PICKED BY YOUR MANAGER FOR THIS PROJECT BECAUSE...

WELL... NEVER MIND WHY.

HERE'S THE BASIC PLAN FOR GETTING OUR "ISO 9000" CERTIFICATION.

EACH OF YOU WILL CREATE AN INSANELY BORING, POORLY WRITTEN DOCUMENT. I'LL COMBINE THEM INTO ONE BIG HONKIN' BINDER.

I'LL SEND COPIES TO ALL DEPARTMENT HEADS FOR COMMENT. THEY WILL TREAT IT LIKE A DEAD RACCOON AND ROUTE IT TO THE FIRST PASSERBY.

THE TRIAL IS GOING BADLY, SO I'M TRYING TO MAKE A DEAL WITH THE DISTRICT ATTORNEY.

HE OFFERED TO GIVE ME A SONY WALKMAN IF YOU WILL ACCEPT THE DEATH PENALTY.

I THINK I CAN GET A WALKMAN FOR YOU, TOO.

I'LL BE REPRESENTING YOU CORPORATE EMPLOYEES IN A CLASS ACTION SUIT. YOUR COMPANY HAS SUCKED THE LIFE FORCE OUT OF YOU AND TURNED YOU INTO LITTLE RAGS.

MY FEE WILL BE ON A CONTINGENCY BASIS. THAT MEANS I GET THE ENTIRE SETTLEMENT PLUS I'LL USE YOU TO WAX MY BMW.

I'VE FOUND THE PERFECT CLIENTS.

SOUNDS FAIR.

DON'T MAKE WAVES.

I'M FROM THE LAW FIRM OF DOGBERT, DOGBERT AND DOGBERT. I'M SUING YOU FOR DRAINING THE LIFE FORCE OUT OF YOUR EMPLOYEES.

AFTER BEING DRAINED OF LIFE, EMPLOYEES ARE FORCED TO LEAVE THE COMPANY. THE LUCKY ONES GET JOBS AS RAGS FOR A CAR WASH, LIKE JOEY PISHKIN HERE.

WHAT JOEY? THAT'S MARGE FROM ACCOUNTING???

HONK HONK

IF YOU DO NOT DROP YOUR CLASS ACTION SUIT, THEN YOU'LL HAVE TO FACE ME IN COURT.

AND I'VE NEVER LOST A CASE.

THEN HOW DO YOU KNOW YOU WOULDN'T ENJOY IT.

WELL... I JUST WOULDN'T.

GOOD ARGUMENT.

BEFORE YOU DECIDE WHO WINS THIS CIVIL SUIT, REMEMBER THIS...

I CAN'T LEGALLY OFFER YOU LARGE CASH KICK-BACKS FOR DECIDING IN MY FAVOR. BUT PLEASE TAKE A MOMENT TO COMPLETE A SELF-ADDRESSED STAMPED ENVELOPE.

WHAT ARE YOU DOING?

I'M TRYING TO ESTABLISH "REASONABLE DOUBT."

THE JURY HAS REACHED A DECISION IN THE CASE OF "DOGBERT VS. A BIG CORPORATION."

WE AWARD DOGBERT FIFTY MILLION DOLLARS BECAUSE WE HATE BIG COMPANIES AND WE LIKE LITTLE DOGS WITH GLASSES.

I HATE MY LIFE.

AND WE AWARD A MAYTAG DRYER TO JUROR MINDY FOR BEING "BEST DRESSED."

I'M AN ATTORNEY FOR MISTER DOGBERT...

HE'S SUING YOU FOR "PETIMONY." YOU ALLEGEDLY PET THE NEIGHBOR'S CAT...

SEE... IT WAS A PAT, NOT A PET. LIKE THIS...

OH LOOK, IT'S "GARFIELD," YOUR FAVORITE...

DOGBERT SUES DILBERT FOR PETIMONY

CAN'T WE HANDLE THIS AMICABLY, WITHOUT LAWYERS?

I'VE BEEN ADVISED THAT YOU'RE UGLY.

I'VE DECIDED TO REJECT YOUR GENEROUS OFFER TO BUY THE COMPANY.

AND IF YOU TRY TO MAKE THIS A HOSTILE TAKEOVER YOU WILL FIND ME TO BE A FORMIDABLE ADVERSARY.

...THEN THEIR LAWYERS CHEWED MY CLOTHES OFF.

JURY SELECTION

MY CLIENT IS ACCUSED OF KILLING TWELVE PEOPLE JUST LIKE YOU FOLKS.

THE ALLEGED VICTIMS WERE ALL PART OF A PREVIOUS JURY WHO DOUBTED MY CLIENT'S INNOCENCE.

THIS JURY IS ACCEPTABLE TO THE DEFENSE.

MY CLIENT HAS BEEN ACCUSED OF THE MOST HEINOUS CRIMES.

BUT DOES THIS LOOK LIKE A PERSON WHO COULD KILL??

OOH! OOH! I KNOW THIS ONE!!

OKAY, LET'S SAY THAT, HYPOTHETICALLY, MY CLIENT DID KILL THOSE PEOPLE...

CHANCES ARE THAT IT WAS NOBODY YOU KNOW.

AND THE NEXT TIME YOU'RE STANDING IN A LONG LINE, ASK YOURSELF: "AM I BETTER OFF NOW THAT THERE ARE LESS PEOPLE?"

LAWYERS

DILBERT *Gives You the Business*

HAS THE JURY REACHED A VERDICT?

YES, YOUR HONOR. WE FIND THE DEFENSE ATTORNEY POORLY DRESSED AND OBNOXIOUS. WE SENTENCE HIM TO DEATH.

I DON'T THINK YOU CAN DO THAT.

FURTHERMORE, WE FIND THAT YOUR HONOR LOOKS FETCHING IN A BLACK MUUMUU.

© 1990 United Feature Syndicate, Inc.

CORRECTION

A RECENT DILBERT STRIP USED THE WORDS "ANT FARM" TO DESCRIBE A HABITAT FOR ANTS.

LAWYERS HAVE INFORMED ME THAT "ANT FARM" IS A TRADEMARK OF "UNCLE MILTON INDUSTRIES, INC." THEY DEMAND A PUBLIC CLARIFICATION.

© 1995 United Feature Syndicate, Inc. (NYC)

WHAT <u>SHOULD</u> WE CALL A HABITAT FOR WORTHLESS AND DISGUSTING LITTLE CREATURES?

LAW SCHOOL.

DILBERT, I'M PUTTING YOU ON A ROTATIONAL ASSIGNMENT...

YOU WILL BE WORKING IN MARKETING UNTIL FURTHER NOTICE.

MARKETING
TWO DRINK MINIMUM

© 1992 United Feature Syndicate, Inc.

DILBERT IS TRANSFERRED TO MARKETING

YOU LOOK LOST.

I NEVER KNEW THAT MARKETING WAS LIKE THIS ... DO YOU PEOPLE DO ANY WORK?

© 1992 United Feature Syndicate, Inc.

WELL, NOT ON "BARBECUE TUESDAY." ARE YOU STAYING FOR LUNCH? IT'S UNICORN!

MARKETING

DILBERT IS TRANSFERRED TO MARKETING

EVERY TUESDAY WE BARBECUE A UNICORN.

MAKE MINE RARE. HA HA! GET IT? RARE?

I'M NOT SURE I BELIEVE THIS IS THE "BEST PART."

WHEN YOU WORK IN MARKETING, YOU USE THE RESEARCH WELL TO TEST NEW IDEAS.

ANY DAY BUT FRIDAY YOU CAN SHOUT YOUR QUESTION INTO THE WELL AND AN ANSWER WILL COME BACK.

WHY NOT FRIDAY?

FRIDAY IS YOUR DAY IN THE WELL.

THINK OF THE COMPANY AS A PERSON. WE IN MARKETING WOULD BE THE "BRAINS."

THE SALES DEPARTMENT WOULD BE THE "BODY."

WHAT'S ENGINEERING?

THE SNOT.

AND THAT'S THE MARKETING PLAN. ANY COMMENTS?

IT APPEARS TO BE A BUNCH OF OBVIOUS GENERALITIES AND WISHFUL THINKING WITH NO APPARENT BUSINESS VALUE.

MARKETING DIDN'T TURN OUT TO BE THE GLAMOUR CAREER I EXPECTED.

I CIRCLED ALL THE WORDS YOU WON'T FIND IN ANY DICTIONARY.

EXPERIMENT #1: I AM EXPOSING A RAT TO MY COMPANY'S MARKETING PLAN.

HE SEEMS TO HAVE NO ADVERSE RESPONSE TO THE INTRODUCTION AND BACKGROUND.

THIS IS ALREADY FAR MORE EXPOSURE THAN HUMANS COULD TOLERATE.

SALES PROJECTIONS... BRAIN TUMOR... GET TYLENOL ...

MAYBE IT WAS WRONG TO PROMISE OUR CUSTOMERS A PRODUCT THAT HASN'T BEEN DESIGNED YET.

BUT OUR MOTTO IN MARKETING IS, "IT'S BETTER TO ASK FOR FORGIVENESS THAN TO SEEK PERMISSION."

YOUR MOTTO NEEDS SOME DESIGN WORK TOO.

EVERYBODY IN ENGINEERING USES THIS PROGRAM I WROTE. I THINK MARKETING SHOULD TURN IT INTO A PRODUCT.

I WOULDN'T BUY THIS.

THAT'S IRRELEVANT BECAUSE THE TARGET MARKET WOULD BE ENGINEERS.

ENGINEERS THINK THE SAME AS MARKETEERS.

IF THAT WERE TRUE WE'D BE SITTING IN A CAVE TRYING TO DECIDE IF ROCKS ARE EDIBLE.

YOU KNOW, YOU COULD KEEP RECIPES ON THIS.

YOUR NEW SOFTWARE IS SUCCESSFULLY INSTALLED. DO YOU WANT TO SEND YOUR REGISTRATION INFO BY MODEM?

YES

THE SOFTWARE HAS FOUND YOUR CREDIT CARD NUMBER AND IS PLACING ORDERS FOR NEW PRODUCTS IT THINKS YOU NEED... PLEASE WAIT.

UH...

MAKING ROOM ON YOUR HARD DRIVE...

I CAN'T TELL IF IT'S A VIRUS OR JUST EXCELLENT MARKETING.

EITHER WAY...

IT'S TIME FOR MARKETING TO PUT THE GLITTER ON THIS SOFTWARE YOU'VE CREATED.

WITH MY GUIDANCE THIS WILL BECOME THE PREMIER DATA BACKUP SOFTWARE!

BEAR IN MIND THAT WE SAID IT WOULD TAKE SIX MONTHS TO WRITE IT.

YOU ONLY GAVE US A MONTH.

WE'LL FIX THE BUGS IN THE NEXT RELEASE.

TELL ME ABOUT THE FEATURES.

AT THIS POINT ALL IT DOES IS ERASE YOUR DISK DRIVE.

UNLESS YOU'RE ON A NETWORK.

WHAT HAPPENS IF YOU'RE ON A NETWORK?

IT ERASES EVERYBODY'S DISK DRIVES.

9/17

AND HEAVEN HELP YOU IF YOU HAVE A MODEM...

IT CALLS ALL YOUR FRIENDS AND ERASES THEIR PCs.

WE'LL CALL IT "QuikProtect."

IF YOU HAVE A SOUND CARD IT SWEARS AT YOU.

ARE YOU INTERESTED IN OUR DIAMOND JEWELRY?

LET ME SEE IF I UNDERSTAND THE CONCEPT HERE...

...I WOULD GIVE YOU THOUSANDS OF DOLLARS, AND IN RETURN...

...YOU WOULD GIVE ME A PEBBLE YOU FOUND ON THE GROUND.

THESE ARE NO ORDINARY PEBBLES. DIAMONDS ARE VERY RARE.

RARE? THAT'S ONLY BECAUSE YOU MADE A MARKETING DECISION TO RESTRICT THE SUPPLY.

OKAY, OKAY, YOU FIGURED US OUT. I'LL GIVE YOU A FREE BAG OF DIAMONDS IF YOU'LL GO AWAY AND KEEP QUIET.

GREAT... NOW I'M A PARTY TO THIS UGLY LITTLE SECRET.

7-12

THE MARKETING DEPARTMENT SAVES THE DAY! CHECK OUT THESE BROCHURES I MADE.

THIS NEW PRODUCT WILL ALLOW US TO DOMINATE THE MARKET!

BUT WE DON'T MAKE THIS PRODUCT.

THAT HASN'T HURT OUR SALES SO FAR.

I'M GOING TO MAKE AN INFOMMERCIAL.

I'M TARGETING THE PEOPLE WHO WANT TO INVEST THEIR SAVINGS BUT DON'T KNOW HOW.

I HOPE YOU PLAN TO SELL EDUCATIONAL INFORMATION ABOUT HOW TO AVOID SCAMS.

GOOD IDEA FOR PHASE TWO!

NOSE PUPPIES! GET YOUR NOSE PUPPIES!

NOSE PUPPIES $1.00

WHAT'S A NOSE PUPPY?

IT'S A LITTLE CERAMIC PUPPY THAT FITS IN YOUR NOSE.

"FIND A NEED AND FILL IT," IS MY MOTTO.

I MAKE THEM MYSELF. EACH ONE IS HAND-PAINTED.

NOSE PUPPIES $1.00

THEY WEREN'T SELLING UNTIL I CAME UP WITH THE CONCEPT OF STICKING THEM UP PEOPLE'S NOSES.

I'M NOT IN IT FOR THE MONEY. I JUST WANT TO LEAVE THIS WORLD A LITTLE BETTER THAN I FOUND IT.

MARKETING

YOU ENGINEERS HAVE DONE <u>NOTHING</u> ON MY PROJECT. YOU JUST KEEP SAYING I HAVEN'T GIVEN YOU SUFFICIENT REQUIREMENTS!

I DON'T KNOW WHAT ELSE YOU NEED AND YOU WON'T TELL ME WHAT YOU NEED!! IS THIS JUST YOUR WAY OF AVOIDING WORK??!

9-8

I'LL BET YOU REGRET CHOOSING MARKETING AS A CAREER PATH.

IT LOOKS LIKE A LOT OF WORK.

© 1993 United Feature Syndicate, Inc.

OKAY, LET'S START BY DOCUMENTING YOUR MARKET REQUIREMENTS.

NO, LET'S START BY YOU TELLING ME ALL THE THINGS YOU CAN DESIGN. THEN I'LL TELL YOU WHICH ONE I LIKE.

WORK CAN BE VERY REWARDING. YOU SHOULD TRY IT.

WHAT'S THAT DOOHICKEY YOU HAVE THERE?

7/3 © 1995 United Feature Syndicate, Inc. (NYC)

HA HA! NOW THAT THE ENGINEERS MUST CHARGE THEIR TIME TO MARKETING, WE <u>OWN</u> YOU!

I'LL JUST REPROGRAM YOUR COMPUTER THROUGH THE LAN SO ITS RADIATION WILL ALTER YOUR DNA.

IS THAT POSSIBLE??!

AS FAR AS YOU KNOW.

7/3 © 1995 United Feature Syndicate, Inc. (NYC)

I TOLD A GUY IN MARKETING THAT I PROGRAMMED HIS COMPUTER TO ALTER HIS DNA STRUCTURE.

HEE HEE

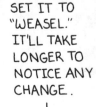

HE THINKS HE'LL TURN INTO SOME KIND OF ANIMAL.

TELL HIM YOU SET IT TO "WEASEL." IT'LL TAKE LONGER TO NOTICE ANY CHANGE.

TELL ME THE TRUTH, ALICE. CAN DILBERT REPROGRAM MY DNA?

YEAH. YOU MARKETING GUYS ONLY HAVE ONE HELIX.

7/4 © 1995 United Feature Syndicate, Inc. (NYC)

MARKETING

MARKETING

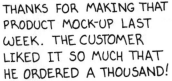

THANKS FOR MAKING THAT PRODUCT MOCK-UP LAST WEEK. THE CUSTOMER LIKED IT SO MUCH THAT HE ORDERED A THOUSAND!

THAT WAS A **MOCK-UP**! WE DON'T MAKE THAT PRODUCT YET. IT WOULD TAKE THREE YEARS TO MAKE ONE.

JUST GIVE ME A THOUSAND MOCK-UPS. THE FIRST ONE WAS TERRIFIC!

THE MOCK-UP WAS OUR COMPETITOR'S PRODUCT WITH DUCT TAPE OVER THE LOGO.

MISTER RATBERT, I DON'T THINK I CAN HIRE A RAT TO BE OUR VICE PRESIDENT OF MARKETING. YOU NEED EXPERIENCE IN THE TECHNOLOGY INDUSTRY.

I SPENT A WEEK IN A DUMPSTER AT PROCTER AND GAMBLE.

CLOSE ENOUGH! WELCOME TO THE TEAM!

I'LL BRING SOME CRONIES WITH ME. THEY'RE FLIES.

I HAD YEARS OF VALUABLE EXPERIENCE AS A RODENT BEFORE I BECAME VICE PRESIDENT OF MARKETING.

MY MARKETING PLAN IS SIMPLE. EACH OF YOU WILL CLING TO THE LEG OF A TECHNOLOGY COLUMNIST UNTIL WE GET SOME GOOD PRESS.

IT LOOKS LIKE YOU'RE FULL.

YOU CAN CLING TO THE CAT UNTIL A SPACE OPENS.

I QUIT MY JOB AS VICE PRESIDENT OF MARKETING...

I WAS LOSING MY SCRUPLES... BECOMING UNSCRUPULOUS. YES, I LEARNED A VALUABLE LESSON ABOUT SCRUPLES.

AND THAT LESSON WOULD BE?

IT'S FUN TO SAY "SCRUPLES."

AT LONG LAST OUR PRODUCT IS COMPLETE. IT SHIPS TOMORROW.

THAT'S TERRIFIC. I ONLY HAVE A FEW ADDITIONAL FEATURES TO ADD AND THE MARKETING DEPARTMENT WILL BE HAPPY.

OKAY

I BELIEVE THAT OUR CUSTOMERS WANT HARDWARE, NOT SOFT-WARE.

IT'S TIMES LIKE THIS I WISH I WERE A PSYCHOPATH.

YOU'RE NOT?

THIS IS VERY TECHNICAL. I'LL EXPLAIN...

SNAP

GALLERY OF GOOGLY-EYED MARKETEERS

DROOL! GOOD ONE.

WE IN ENGINEERING THINK OF THE MARKETING DEPART-MENT AS OUR CUSTOMER, FRED.

THAT'S GREAT. I'D LIKE YOU TO DO A TECHNICAL FEASI-BILITY STUDY FOR ME.

3-7

WOULD THAT REQUIRE ANY WORK?

I SAID "CUSTOMER," NOT "BOSS."

WHAT SHALL WE TELL THE GUY FROM MARKETING THIS TIME?

Hee Hee

LET'S SEE IF WE CAN MAKE HIM FEEL A SENSE OF HELPLESS DESPERATION AND FEAR.

THE TIME-DIVISION MULTIPLEXER OPENED A HOLE IN THE FABRIC OF SPACE.

WE'RE TRAPPED IN THIS MEETING FOREVER.

BOB, YOUR SELF-ESTEEM MIGHT IMPROVE IF YOU GOT A JOB.

AS WHAT?

THERE'S AN OPENING IN OUR PROCUREMENT DEPARTMENT. YOU'D BE PERFECT.

WHAT DOES PROCURE-MENT DO?

THEIR JOB IS TO PREVENT US FROM GETTING THE COMPUTERS WE WANT.

CAN I HIT PEOPLE WITH MY TAIL?

7/27 © 1995 United Feature Syndicate, Inc. (NYC)

BOB WORKS IN PROCUREMENT

YOUR DUTIES ARE SIMPLE. PEOPLE WILL COME TO YOU AND ASK FOR THINGS.

ASSUME ALL EMPLOYEES ARE LYING, TREASURE-HUNTING THIEVES. GIVE THEM LOW-COST SUB-STITUTES AND CLAIM THE SAVINGS ON YOUR ACCOMPLISHMENTS.

I ASKED FOR A MULTIMEDIA LAPTOP PC. THIS IS A "DYMO" LABELER.

NICE TRY, PAUL, IF THAT'S YOUR REAL NAME.

7/28 © 1995 United Feature Syndicate, Inc. (NYC)

BOB IN PROCUREMENT

I'M AFRAID THE EQUIP-MENT YOU WANT IS NOT ON THE APPROVED EQUIPMENT LIST.

LET ME THINK... IF I ADD THIS TO THE APPROVED LIST, THAT'S MORE WORK FOR ME... BUT IF I SAY NO, IT'S MORE WORK FOR YOU... HMM...THINK, THINK...

I'D LIKE TO SEE THIS ALLEGED LIST.

WELL, IT'S NOT SO MUCH A PHYSICAL LIST AS IT IS A PHILOSOPHY.

7/29 © 1995 United Feature Syndicate, Inc. (NYC)

WHEN I STARTED PROGRAMMING, WE DIDN'T HAVE ANY OF THESE SISSY "ICONS" AND "WINDOWS."

ALL WE HAD WERE ZEROS AND ONES -- AND SOMETIMES WE DIDN'T EVEN HAVE ONES.

I WROTE AN ENTIRE DATABASE PROGRAM USING ONLY ZEROS.

YOU HAD ZEROS? WE HAD TO USE THE LETTER "O."

© 1992 United Feature Syndicate, Inc.

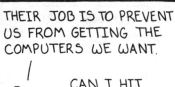

I COULDN'T HELP NOTICING THE BUGS IN THE PROGRAM ON THIS OLD DISKETTE YOU THREW AWAY.

I FIXED THE BUGS AND TIGHTENED THE CODE FROM TWELVE THOUSAND LINES TO SIXTEEN.

IT TOOK ME THREE MONTHS TO WRITE THAT PROGRAM.

I TOOK THE LIBERTY OF UPDATING YOUR RESUME. I'M GUESSING YOU'LL NEED IT SOON.

I DON'T HAVE ANY MEETINGS TODAY.

I'LL CHANGE ALL MY SOFTWARE SETTINGS UNTIL SOMETHING DOESN'T WORK.

KEEP UP THE GOOD WORK.

KEEP UP THE GOOD MANAGING.

WALLY WRITES THE CRITICAL CODE FOR OUR NATION'S NEW AIR TRAFFIC CONTROL SYSTEM.

THE CROWD IS SILENT.

SUDDENLY THE GIFTED PROGRAMMER EMPLOYS A RARELY SEEN STRATEGY OF "CODE REUSE."

THE CROWD GOES WILD.

SO YOU USED CODE FROM THE PAYROLL SYSTEM?

HERE'S A TIP: DON'T FLY ON PAY DAY.

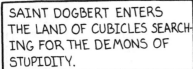

SAINT DOGBERT ENTERS THE LAND OF CUBICLES SEARCHING FOR THE DEMONS OF STUPIDITY.

SUDDENLY HE FINDS AN OVER-PROMOTED COMPUTER GURU SPOUTING USELESS DATABASE CONCEPTS.

YOU'D BE FOOLS TO IGNORE THE BOOLEAN ANTI-BINARY LEAST-SQUARE APPROACH.

THE MONSTER IS DISPATCHED TO THE DARK WORLD BY THE SIGHT OF ITS MOST FEARED OBJECT.

LOOK! ACTUAL CODE!

COOL!

  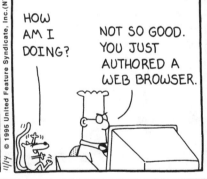

I HEARD THAT OUR SOFTWARE DEVELOPMENT WORK HAS BEEN MOVED TO THE TINY NATION OF ELBONIA.

THINGS CAN'T GET WORSE THAN THAT.

DILBERT, YOU'RE IN CHARGE OF INTEGRATING THE ELBONIAN'S SOFTWARE WITH OUR EXISTING SYSTEMS.

OKAY, NOW IT CAN'T GET ANY WORSE.

YOU MIGHT WANT TO GET A TUBERCULOSIS VACCINATION.

SOMEWHERE IN ELBONIA

I'VE BEEN ASSIGNED TO CHECK THE SOFTWARE YOU'RE WRITING FOR US UNDER CONTRACT.

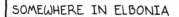

THE DOCUMENTATION IS WRITTEN IN OUR OWN ELBONIAN LANGUAGE.

IS THAT A PROBLEM?

THAT'S BETTER THAN I'D HOPED. I WAS AFRAID NOBODY HERE KNEW HOW TO WRITE.

WRITING IS EASY. SOMEDAY WE HOPE TO READ, TOO.

BEFORE I ACCEPT THE SOFTWARE YOU WROTE UNDER CONTRACT, TELL ME WHAT DEVELOPMENT METHODOLOGY YOU USE.

WE HOLD VILLAGE MEETINGS TO BOAST OF OUR SKILLS AND CURSE THE DEVIL-SPAWNED END-USERS.

SOMETIMES WE JUGGLE.

AT THE LAST MINUTE WE SLAM OUT SOME CODE AND GO ROLLER SKATING.

I WOULD FIND THIS HUMOROUS IF NOT FOR THE PIG ON MY BACK.

YOU SAVED ONE MILLION DOLLARS BY HAVING PROGRAMMERS IN ELBONIA WRITE SOFTWARE FOR US.

BUT WE WASTED FOUR MILLION DOLLARS TRYING TO DEBUG THE SOFTWARE.

AND THE ENTIRE STAFF OF OUR QUALITY ASSURANCE GROUP QUIT TO BECOME MIMES.

LET'S BLAME THE MIMES; THEY WON'T TALK.

WHAT THE...?

YOU RESPOND TOO QUICKLY TO MY E-MAIL.

OBVIOUSLY YOU AREN'T FOCUSING ON PRIORITIES.

I DO E-MAIL WHILE MY PROGRAM IS COMPILING.

YOU CAN'T WEASEL OUT OF THIS WITH YOUR TECHNICAL MUMBO JUMBO.

© 1998 United Feature Syndicate, Inc.

YOU WIN. I'LL IGNORE YOUR E-MAIL FROM NOW ON.

THE IMPORTANT THING IS THAT I WIN.

I WONDER IF MY PROGRAMS EVER COMPILE.

IT'S TIME TO END THIS CHARADE, ZIMBU!

YOUR LANGUAGE SKILLS ARE SIMPLE ROTE BEHAVIOR. MONKEYS ARE INCAPABLE OF LOGIC AND REASONING.

© 1991 United Feature Syndicate, Inc.

HA! AND THAT PROGRAM YOU'RE WRITING -- IT'S PROBABLY IN "BASIC."

DO YOU EVER WORK?

I THINK WE SHOULD BUILD AN SQL DATABASE.

UH-OH

DOES HE UNDERSTAND WHAT HE SAID OR IS IT SOMETHING HE SAW IN A TRADE MAGAZINE AD?

© 1995 United Feature Syndicate, Inc. (NYC)

WHAT COLOR DO YOU WANT THAT DATABASE?

I THINK MAUVE HAS THE MOST RAM.

 PETER, YOU'RE A BRILLIANT COMPUTER PROGRAMMER AND YOU LIKE YOUR JOB.

 ALTHOUGH YOU LACK ANY SOCIAL AWARENESS AND CANNOT COMMUNICATE WITH YOUR SPECIES, I DECIDED TO PROMOTE YOU TO MANAGEMENT.

 DON'T BE AFRAID... IT'S CALLED A NECKTIE.

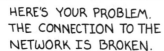 OKAY, JUST SHOW ME HOW TO PROGRAM SO I CAN HELP OUT ON YOUR PROJECT.

 YOU'RE GOING TO BUILD A "G.U.I." USING OBJECT-ORIENTED DEVELOPMENT TOOLS...

G.U.I. IS PRONOUNCED "GOOEY."

 I USED MY GUN OBJECT TO BLAST THE BUG OBJECT IN THE HALL OBJECT!!

NOTICE HOW GOOEY IT IS.

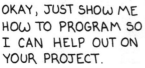 HERE'S YOUR PROBLEM. THE CONNECTION TO THE NETWORK IS BROKEN.

 UH-OH. IT'S A "TOKEN RING" LAN. THAT MEANS THE TOKEN FELL OUT AND IT'S IN THIS ROOM SOMEPLACE.

 YOU ARE THE WIND BENEATH MY WINGS.

I'LL WAIT A WEEK THEN TELL HIM THE TOKEN MUST BE IN THE "ETHERNET."

 WE HAD TO CUT SOME CORNERS TO GET THE DEMO READY THIS SOON.

 WALLY IS UNDER THE TABLE. HE'LL PRETEND TO BE THE 3-D INTERFACE THAT WE COULD BUILD IF WE WEREN'T DOING USELESS DEMOS.

 HE'S A LITTLE FUZZY. CAN YOU ADJUST IT?

TRY THE ELECTRIC SHAVER.

Panel 1:
OUR NEW VP IS COMING. IS THE DEMO OF OUR HOLO-GRAPHIC INTERFACE READY?

Panel 2:
EVERYTHING SHOULD BE FINE... UNLESS WE'RE SUDDENLY VISITED BY THE DARK ANGEL OF PRODUCT DEMOS...

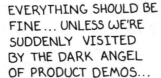

Panel 3:
HELLO-O-O, WALLY. DID SOMEBODY SAY "DEMO"?

I'M DILBERT; LOYAL PEON.

© 1996 United Feature Syndicate, Inc. (NYC)

Panel 4:
WE PLANNED A DAZZLING DEMO FOR YOU, BUT AS YOU CAN SEE WE'RE BEING VISITED BY THE DARK ANGEL OF DEMOS.

Panel 5:
THE DEMO IS A SHAM. THEIR PROJECT IS DOOMED. CUT THEIR FUNDING BEFORE YOUR NAME IS ASSOCIATED WITH IT.

© 1996 United Feature Syndicate, Inc. (NYC)

Panel 6:
THE WORST IS OVER.

LOOK AT SOME OF THE PICTURES THE "BOYS" STORE ON THE FILE SERVER.

Panel 7:
I DECLARE MYSELF THE PATRON SAINT OF TECHNOLOGY.

1-31

Panel 8:
I HEAL BROKEN TECH-NOLOGY WITH MY RIGHT PAW AND I USE THE SCEPTER TO DRIVE OUT THE DEMONS OF STUPIDITY.

© 1994 United Feature Syndicate, Inc.

Panel 9:
I DON'T THINK I'VE SEEN YOUR SPIRITUAL SIDE BEFORE.

OUT!

OUT!

Panel 10:
SAINT DOGBERT SEEKS OUT TECHNOLOGY THAT HAS BEEN POSSESSED BY THE DEMONS OF STUPIDITY.

2-1

Panel 11:
HE HAPPENS ACROSS A SOFTWARE DEVELOPER.

I'LL MAKE THE COMMAND EASY TO REMEMBER, LIKE "CTRL-ALT-F4-DEL".

© 1994 United Feature Syndicate, Inc.

Panel 12:
AND IF THEY FORGET THAT THEY CAN JUST EDIT THE SOURCE CODE IN "COMMAND.COM"

PERFECT.

OUT! OUT!

I'D LIKE TO KICK-OFF THE PROJECT WITH THE TRADITIONAL BAD-MOUTHING OF THE GUY WHO WORKED ON THIS BEFORE.

HE'S SO SLIMY THAT SLUGS POUR SALT ON HIM. HIS BRAIN WOULD RATTLE IN A FLEA'S SKULL!

OH, AND I'LL NEED YOUR FILES.

FLEAS DON'T HAVE "SKULLS"!!

AS YOU KNOW, ALL PROJECTS ARE ASSIGNED ACRONYMS. UNFORTUNATELY, ALL THE GOOD ONES HAVE BEEN USED.

ANY NEW PROJECT WILL HAVE TO USE AN ACRONYM FROM THIS SHORT LIST OF SOMEWHAT LESS DESIRABLE CHOICES.

WHAT SHOULD I CALL MY NEW PROJECT?

WELL, YOU COULD USE "PHLEGM" OR "PLACENTA."

YESTERDAY WE RAN OUT OF ACRONYMS. TODAY WE USED OUR LAST ACCOUNTING CODE. WE'RE IN BIG TROUBLE.

WHY DON'T WE JUST REPROGRAM THE COMPUTERS TO ACCEPT LONGER CODES?

A PROJECT LIKE THAT WOULD NEED AN ACRONYM AND AN ACCOUNTING CODE.

WHY NOT REUSE A CODE FROM A PROJECT THAT'S COMPLETE?

ODDLY ENOUGH, WE'VE NEVER COMPLETED A PROJECT.

TERRIBLE NEWS: MY BOSS ASSIGNED ME TO A FUN AND VALUABLE PROJECT.

UH-OH. THAT MEANS AT LEAST THREE MORONS WILL BE ASSIGNED TO SIMILAR PROJECTS. YOU MUST FIND THEM AND CRUSH THEM...

EXACTLY.

CARL, OLD BUDDY, WHATCHA WORKIN' ON THESE DAYS?

NOTHING FUN AND VALUABLE. SHOO SHOO!!

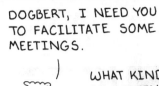

DOGBERT, I NEED YOU TO FACILITATE SOME MEETINGS.

WHAT KIND OF MEETINGS?

WE'RE CREATING A PROCESS TO FIX OUR PRODUCT DEVELOPMENT PROCESS. BUT FIRST WE'RE HAVING SOME PREPLANNING MEETINGS...

...TO DECIDE ON A PROJECT NAME.

HOW ABOUT "DEATH SPIRAL"?

I PUT TOGETHER A TIME LINE FOR YOUR PROJECT.

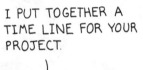

I STARTED BY REASONING THAT ANYTHING I DON'T UNDERSTAND IS EASY TO DO.

PHASE ONE: DESIGN A CLIENT-SERVER ARCHITECTURE FOR OUR WORLD-WIDE OPERATIONS. TIME: SIX MINUTES.

AT FIRST I THOUGHT YOU COMMITTED ME TO AN IMPOSSIBLE DEADLINE. BUT I HAVE A THEORETICAL SOLUTION.

IT INVOLVES FLYING AROUND THE EARTH SO FAST THAT I TRAVEL BACK TO THE PAST.

AND THEN YOU'LL HAVE ENOUGH TIME?

NO, THEN I'LL GIVE YOUR PARENTS THIS PAMPHLET ON CONTRACEPTION.

I HAD TO MAKE SOME OPTIMISTIC ASSUMPTIONS TO MEET THE REVENUE TARGET.

IN WEEK THREE, WE'RE VISITED BY AN ALIEN NAMED D'UTOX INAG WHO OFFERS TO SHARE HIS ADVANCED TECHNOLOGY.

THEN DO WE USE HIS TECHNOLOGY TO DESIGN OUR NEW PRODUCT?

NO, WE KILL HIM AND SELL THE AUTOPSY VIDEO.

I'VE DECIDED TO GET MORE INVOLVED WITH YOUR PROJECT.

UH-OH.

UH-OH.

I'M JUST GOING TO ROLL UP MY SLEEVES AND PITCH IN.

DOES ANYBODY KNOW HOW TO WORK THESE BUTTONS?

OUR ORIGINAL PROJECT TIME LINE WAS TWELVE MONTHS... BUT SINCE YOU PITCHED IN TO HELP...

I DON'T HAVE AN EXACT END DATE, BUT IT'S ROUGHLY THE SAME TIME THAT THE SUN BECOMES A COLD DARK CHUNK OF COAL THE SIZE OF YOUR FOREHEAD.

WE'LL NEED FLASH-LIGHTS.

AND SWEATERS. IT COULD GET NIPPY.

THE PROBLEM...

WE'RE SO UNDER-STAFFED THAT THE PROJECT IS SIX WEEKS BEHIND SCHEDULE.

THE ANALYSIS...

I CAN'T ADD PEOPLE... I CAN'T CHANGE THE DUE DATE... I CAN'T IGNORE IT.

THE RESULT...

HE WANTS DAILY STATUS REPORTS UNTIL THE SITUATION IMPROVES.

I COULD GIVE YOU MARKETING'S APPROVAL RIGHT NOW...

OR I COULD FLEX MY VICE PRESIDENTIAL POWER AND SEND YOU TO GATHER MORE USELESS DATA... MY EGO WOULD EXPAND AND I'D BE A MAJOR STALLION WITH MY WIFE TONIGHT.

DO YOU THINK YOU CAN TOP THAT?

I'LL TRY, SIR. WHAT'S YOUR WIFE'S ADDRESS?

I NEED YOUR APPROVAL ON MY BUSINESS CASE, TOM.

I'LL WEDGE IT IN HERE SO YOU CAN CLAIM YOU NEVER SAW IT WHEN I ASK ABOUT IT NEXT WEEK.

THANKS

THE WEIRD PART IS THAT I CAN FEEL PRODUCTIVE EVEN WHEN I'M DOOMED.

TODAY I DISTRIBUTED 36 COPIES OF MY BUSINESS CASE TO VARIOUS MANAGERS FOR APPROVAL.

BY MY COUNT, 20 ARE BEING MISPLACED, 6 MANAGERS WILL TRY TO KILL IT FOR PERSONAL GAIN AND 10 WILL COME BACK WITH IRRELEVANT QUESTIONS.

WHEN I DIE I WANT TO BE BURIED, NOT CREMATED, SO I CAN AT LEAST MAKE ONE LASTING IMPRESSION ON THE EARTH.

I WAS PLANNING TO MAIL YOUR CORPSE TO SOMEBODY I DON'T LIKE.

THANKS TO MY LEADERSHIP, THE NEW AIR TRAFFIC CONTROL SYSTEM IS DESIGNED ON TIME AND UNDER BUDGET.

I HAD TO CUT A FEW CORNERS. THIS BIG RADAR-LOOKING THING IS A WALL CLOCK. AND MOST OF THE BUTTONS ARE GLUED ON.

IT LOOKS LIKE IT MIGHT BE UM... DANGEROUS.

GREAT... I FINISH EARLY AND WHAT DO I GET: "FEATURE CREEP."

I HAVE DISCOVERED THE CAUSE OF YOUR PROJECT DELAYS.

SOMEBODY IN THIS ROOM IS A PIECE OF DEADWOOD PRETENDING TO BE A CONTRIBUTOR!

IT IS YOU!

HEY, I MADE SOME CALLS AND I'M WAITING FOR INFORMATION!

I'M PUTTING YOU IN CHARGE OF PROJECT "BIFF."

DILBERT

"BIFF" STANDS FOR "BIG IMPROVEMENTS FOR FREE."

YOUR JOB IS TO RECOMMEND WAYS TO INCREASE PROFITS WITHOUT SPENDING MONEY OR CHANGING ANYTHING.

YOU HAVE TO SPEND MONEY TO MAKE MONEY.

IF WE HAD MONEY TO SPEND WE WOULDN'T NEED TO MAKE MONEY.

DUH

THE POINT IS THAT YOU CAN MAKE MORE MONEY THAN YOU SPEND.

I'M NOT FOLLOWING YOUR SO-CALLED "POINT."

LOGICALLY, ANYTHING I DON'T UNDERSTAND IS UNIMPORTANT.

HAVE YOUR REPORT TOMORROW.

SO, YOU RECOMMEND... REPLACING ALL MANAGERS WITH LAVA LAMPS.

HERE'S A FEW BUCKS FOR THE LAVA LAMPS.

TAKE CARE OF THIS, ALICE.

"TAKE CARE OF THIS"? THIS WOULD DOUBLE MY WORKLOAD.

I'VE ALREADY GOT SO MANY PROJECTS THAT I CAN'T DO ANYTHING USEFUL WITH ANY OF THEM.

BUT IF SUCCESS IS IMPOSSIBLE THEN...

I'M...FREE.

FREE! FREE! HA HA HA HA HA

THE RESULT WILL BE THE SAME NO MATTER WHAT I DO! ♫ YES YES YES

HONK HONK!

MOVING ALONG...WE NEED TO INVENTORY OUR OFFICE EQUIP-MENT.

SOUNDS LIKE A JOB FOR ALICE.

DILBERT *Gives You the Business*

COULD YOU DO A DEMO OF THE NEW PRODUCT FOR OUR VP NEXT WEEK?

WELL... THAT WOULD DELAY THE SHIP DATE, LOWER MORALE AND CREATE AN UNENDING DEMAND FOR MORE UNPRODUCTIVE DEMOS...

LOGICALLY, SINCE YOUR OBJECTIVE IS TO SHOW THAT WE'RE DOING VALUABLE WORK...

AND WE'LL NEED A BANNER THAT SAYS "QUALITY."

YOUR NEW PROJECT WILL HAVE NO BUDGET AND NO MANAGEMENT SUPPORT. EXPECT TO SPEND MOST OF YOUR TIME GIVING STATUS REPORTS.

OH NO! THE LIFE FORCE HAS BEEN DRAINED OUT OF ME! I'M BECOMING A DAMP RAG!!!

THAT'S AMAZING.

IT'S NOTHING. I DID EIGHTEEN AT ONCE AT THE EMPLOYEE EMPOWERMENT BRUNCH.

AT THIS PHASE, THE PROJECT WILL BE REVIEWED BY A WORTHLESS MANAGER.

HEE-HEE! I WONDER IF HE KNOWS WHAT PEOPLE SAY ABOUT HIM.

WHY ARE YOU MARKING IT "DONE"? DID YOU DECIDE TO SKIP THAT PHASE?

I'M THE RAG MAN FROM PROJECT LUSER.

BUDGET CUTS HAVE HIT OUR PROJECT HARD. I'M FORCED TO BEG FOR RESOURCES.

I CAN SPARE SOME PENCIL SHAVINGS.

EXCELLENT! WE MAKE COFFEE OUT OF THAT.

CAN YOU SPARE ANY OFFICE SUPPLIES? I'M ON AN UNDERFUNDED PROJECT.

HOW ABOUT A THREE-RING BINDER WITH ONE RING?

SCORE!

I'LL MELT INTO THE BACKGROUND AND LET YOU GET BACK TO YOUR PALACE AND YOUR FANCY COFFEE.

IT'S A MOCHA.

I HATE BEING ON AN UNDERFUNDED PROJECT.

CAN YOU SPARE SOME RESOURCES, LADY? HOW ABOUT THAT INTERN? ARE YOU USING HIM?

FIRST YOU HAVE TO LEARN HOW TO GIVE YOURSELF A SPONGE BATH AT THE WATER FOUNTAIN.

I TOLD YOU THIS PROJECT WOULD TAKE A YEAR. BUT ON MY OBJECTIVES YOU SAY I MUST HAVE IT DONE IN THREE MONTHS.

WHICH OF THESE REASONS BEST DESCRIBES WHY:
A. YOU HAVE GREAT CONFIDENCE IN ME.
B. YOU THINK I PADDED MY ESTIMATE.
C. YOU HATE MY GUTS.

WE DON'T REALLY NEED THE PROJECT. IT'S JUST A WAY TO KEEP RAISES LOW.

I JUST FELT A LITTLE DIP IN MY MOTIVATION.

WALLY, I'VE DECIDED TO MOVE YOUR PROJECT DUE DATE UP A MONTH.

EVERY TIME IT LOOKS LIKE I'LL REACH AN OBJECTIVE, YOU MOVE IT! WHAT DOES THIS PROVE ABOUT MY PERFORMANCE?

IT PROVES I'M BETTER AT SETTING OBJECTIVES THAN YOU ARE AT ACHIEVING THEM.

© 1998 United Feature Syndicate, Inc.
3/27/98
© 1998 United Feature Syndicate, Inc.
3/29/98
2/8/96 © 1996 United Feature Syndicate, Inc. (NYC)
2/9/96 © 1996 United Feature Syndicate, Inc. (NYC)

DILBERT *Gives You the Business*

WE DESPERATELY NEED ANOTHER PERSON ON MY PROJECT!

WE'RE ALREADY OVER HEADCOUNT. GET A CONTRACT EMPLOYEE.

OKAY, BUT THEY COST TWICE AS MUCH.

PLUS WE NEED TO BUY A COMPUTER.

RENT ONE. WE'RE OVER OUR CAPITAL BUDGET.

RENTING IS EXPENSIVE. WE'LL GO OVER OUR EXPENSE BUDGET.

I'LL FIRE WALLY. THAT WILL FREE UP SOME CASH.

WALLY'S ON MY PROJECT!

FORGET IT! I'LL JUST WORK SIXTEEN HOURS A DAY!!

THAT WORKED OUT PERFECTLY. I THINK I MIGHT BE A GENIUS OR SOMETHING.

I WONDER IF I SHOULD HAVE TOLD HIM THE PROJECT WAS CANCELLED LAST WEEK.

© 1995 United Feature Syndicate, Inc.

WE JUST HIRED JACK AWAY FROM OUR COMPETITOR. HE WAS THEIR BEST MANAGER.

JACK WILL BE IN CHARGE OF PROJECT "GOOSEFOOD."

I'D LIKE YOU TWO TO BRIEF JACK ON THE PROJECT.

PROJECT "GOOSEFOOD" HAS NO BUDGET AND NO MANAGEMENT SUPPORT.

YOUR JOB IS TO BUILD A GLOBAL INFORMATION NETWORK IN TWO WEEKS.

© 1995 United Feature Syndicate, Inc. (NYC)

FAILURE IS CERTAIN. SOON YOU WILL LEAVE THE INDUSTRY IN DISGRACE.

... JUST LIKE THE OTHER "BEST MANAGERS" WE HIRED FROM OUR COMPETITORS.

JUST OUT OF CURIOSITY, HOW DID THE PROJECT GET ITS NAME?

LET'S JUST SAY THAT YOU'RE THE GOOSE FOOD...

THE PROJECT STATUS IS "YELLOW LIGHT."

IN USER TESTS WE FOUND THAT THE PRODUCT LOCKS UP EVERY TWELVE SECONDS. THE INTERFACE IS INCOMPREHENSIBLE AND THE MANUAL IS PURE FICTION.

I THINK IT'S CLEAR WHAT WE NEED TO DO...

SHIP IT AND HOPE SOMEBODY WRITES A "DUMMIES" BOOK ABOUT IT?

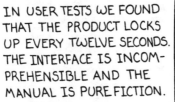

IT LOOKS LIKE WE'LL RELEASE OUR NEW PRODUCT ON TIME, DESPITE ITS MANY DEFECTS.

WE'VE MINIMIZED THE ECONOMIC IMPACT OF THE DEFECTS VIA AN ADVANCED BUSINESS PROCESS CALLED "HOPING NOBODY NOTICES."

AND WE'VE DOUBLED OUR PROJECTED INCOME BY MODIFYING OUR ASSUMPTIONS!

A LOT OF THIS JOB IS MENTAL.

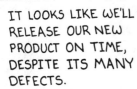
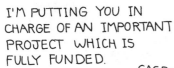

I'M PUTTING YOU IN CHARGE OF AN IMPORTANT PROJECT WHICH IS FULLY FUNDED.

GASP

I'M A MARKED MAN. THE OTHER EMPLOYEES WILL EITHER TRY TO SUCK UP TO ME FOR MONEY OR THROW BRICKS AT ME.

BUDDY!

THE TRICK IS TO KEEP A PROTECTIVE RING OF SUCK-UPS AROUND AT ALL TIMES.

ZIP!

THANK YOU ALL FOR COMING TO THE PROJECT KICK-OFF MEETING.

AS PROJECT MANAGER I'VE DECIDED TO NOT TELL YOU THE PURPOSE OF THE PROJECT. THAT WAY IT WILL BE HARDER FOR YOU TO SABOTAGE IT.

DOES IT REQUIRE ANY SUPERFAST MICROCHIPS?

GOOD LORD, NO. DON'T BUILD ANY OF THOSE... BY TUESDAY.

DILBERT *Gives You the Business*

HOW'S YOUR PROJECT COMING ALONG?

IT'S UNDER-FUNDED AND DOOMED. BUT I'VE GOT SOME GOOD INERTIA GOING AND I'M SETTING THE MARKETING DEPARTMENT UP TO TAKE THE BLAME.

5-20

I FEEL LIKE I SHOULD BE DOING SOMETHING HERE.

I'VE GOT YOU PLANNED TO MAKE AN UNINFORMED DECISION NEXT WEEK.

WE JUST HAD A MEETING AND DECIDED TO CHANGE YOUR PROJECT SUBSTANTIALLY.

WE DIDN'T INVITE YOU TO THE MEETING BECAUSE THINGS GO SMOOTHER WHEN NOBODY HAS ANY ACTUAL KNOWLEDGE.

5-21

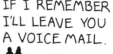 

SO, WHAT ARE THE CHANGES?

IF I REMEMBER I'LL LEAVE YOU A VOICE MAIL.

I WAS JUST READING YOUR PROJECT STATUS REPORT.

YOU SAY THE PROJECT IS DELAYED "DUE TO THE ONGOING BUNGLING OF A CLUELESS, POINTY-HAIR INDIVIDUAL."

5-24

INSTEAD OF SAYING "DUE TO," IT WOULD READ BETTER AS "FACILITATED BY."

I'M CANCELING YOUR PROJECT SO I CAN GIVE YOUR FUNDING TO A PROJECT THAT HAS A MUCH COOLER ACRONYM.

5-25

HA! THE JOKE'S ON YOU! I ANTICIPATED THIS MOVE FROM THE BEGINNING AND HAVE DONE NOTHING BUT CARRY EMPTY BINDERS FOR WEEKS!

BEING GOOD AT YOUR JOB IS LESS FULFILLING THAN YOU MIGHT THINK, DOGBERT.

RATBERT, MY COMPANY IS HIRING FOR OUR QUALITY ASSURANCE GROUP. YOU'D BE PERFECT.

WHAT WOULD I HAVE TO DO?

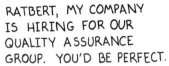

YOU WOULD FIND FLAWS IN OUR NEW PRODUCT, THUS MAKING YOURSELF AN OBJECT OF INTENSE HATRED AND RIDICULE.

BUT THEN YOU'D FIX THOSE FLAWS... AND YOUR RESPECT FOR ME WOULD GROW INTO A SPECIAL BOND OF FRIENDSHIP, RIGHT?!

NO, THEN WE SHIP.

I'D BE PERFECT FOR THE JOB IN QUALITY ASSURANCE. HERE'S MY RESUME.

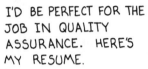

ARE YOU BOTHERED BY THE FACT THAT HALF OF YOUR WORDS ARE SPELLED WRONG?

NOPE! I'M NOT EVEN BOTHERED BY YOUR ANAL-RETENTIVE BEHAVIOR.

YOU'RE HIRED. YOUR BONUS WILL EQUAL NEGATIVE 100% OF YOUR BASE SALARY. OKAY?

I DON'T SEE ANY PROBLEM WITH THAT.

MY QUALITY ASSURANCE REVIEW OF YOUR BETA PRODUCT TURNED UP A FEW BUGS, WALLY.

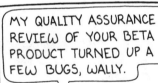

I'VE CLASSIFIED THE BUGS BY SEVERITY: 1) LETHAL, 2) BONEHEADED, 3) VEXING.

ALL I SEE ARE LETHAL AND VEXING. WHERE'S BONEHEADED?

I'M TRYING TO RENT A STADIUM TO HOLD THE PRINTOUT.

IN THE SHORT TIME YOU'VE WORKED IN QUALITY ASSURANCE, YOU'VE FOUND A HUGE NUMBER OF FLAWS IN OUR PROTOTYPE.

THAT'S MY JOB!

YOU'RE JEOPARDIZING OUR SCHEDULE. THE ENTIRE PROJECT WILL FAIL AND IT'S ALL YOUR FAULT.

WHY IS IT MY FAULT?

IF A TREE FALLS IN THE FOREST... AND WE'VE ALREADY SOLD THE TREE... DOES IT HAVE QUALITY?

HOW MANY ANGELS CAN DANCE ON YOUR HEAD?

S. Adams

© 1996 United Feature Syndicate, Inc. (NYC)
7/1/96
7/2/96
7/3/96
7/4/96

RETAIL AND SERVICE JOBS

DRY CLEANING WHILE YOU WAIT

WE'LL HAVE IT DONE IN THREE DAYS.

THE SIGN SAYS "WHILE YOU WAIT."

DO YOU THINK YOU'LL STOP WAITING AFTER TWO DAYS?

NO, YOU FOOL. THAT MODEM WILL NEVER FIT YOUR NEED.

THE SPECS LOOK OKAY.

YOU'RE AN IDIOT COMPARED TO ME! PUT THAT DOWN! IT'S THE WRONG INTERFACE! THE WRONG INTERFACE!!!

IS HE ON COMMISSION?

YEAH, HE PAYS US A DOLLAR PER CUSTOMER.

RRRR

BEFORE I CHECK YOU IN, LET ME EXPLAIN SOMETHING ...

YOU'RE HERE FOR A TECHNOLOGY CONFERENCE. I AM THE ONLY ATTRACTIVE WOMAN WHO WILL TALK TO YOU FOR DAYS. I AM NOT FREE FOR COFFEE LATER.

CAN I BRUSH YOUR HAND WHEN YOU GIVE ME THE KEY?

I'LL TOSS IT TO YOU.

CAN YOU HELP ME?

NO, I'M AFRAID I CAN'T.

SALE

YOU SEE, I GET PAID THE SAME LOW HOURLY WAGE WHETHER YOU BUY THAT SHIRT OR NOT. AND AFTER YEARS IN THIS BUSINESS I'VE LEARNED TO DESPISE THE GENERAL PUBLIC.

PLEASE... I HAVE EXACT CHANGE.

I HAVE NO WAY OF KNOWING IF THAT'S TRUE.

DILBERT *Gives You the Business*

RETAIL AND SERVICE JOBS

120

THE ROOF IS LEAKING THERE. CAN YOU FIX IT TOMORROW?

WELL, LIKE ALL MEMBERS OF MY PROFESSION, I'M UNRELIABLE. HOWEVER, I COULD GIVE YOU A QUOTE AND THEN NEVER SHOW UP OR RETURN YOUR CALLS.

YOU'RE HIRED. NOBODY ELSE WOULD EVEN SHOW UP FOR THE QUOTE.

I DEPEND ON REPEAT CUSTOMERS.

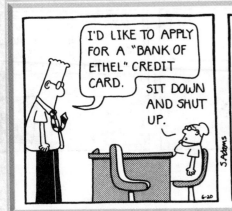

I'D LIKE TO APPLY FOR A "BANK OF ETHEL" CREDIT CARD.

SIT DOWN AND SHUT UP.

IT'S 21% INTEREST PLUS SURPRISINGLY HIGH ANNUAL FEES. WE'LL DO A CREDIT CHECK AND A FULL BODY CAVITY SEARCH.

...AND I HAD TO SMILE THE WHOLE TIME BECAUSE THEY WERE FILMING IT FOR THEIR TELEVISION ADS.

YOU HAVE TO ADMIRE THEIR ATTITUDE.

IT'S NICE, BUT THE WEASEL DOWN THE STREET IS SELLING IT FOR LESS.

YOU SHOULD NEVER SETTLE FOR THE LESSER OF TWO WEASELS.

NOW THAT YOU MENTION IT, IT DID SEEM TOO CONVENIENT.

I CANNOT ALLOW THIS WITHDRAWAL...

BANK OF ETHEL

UNLESS YOU DEFEAT ME IN HAND TO HAND COMBAT.

THEY SEEM PRETTY SERIOUS ABOUT ENCOURAGING THE USE OF THEIR AUTOMATED TELLER MACHINES.

RETAIL AND SERVICE JOBS

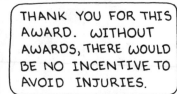

I'M WITH THE CUBICLE POLICE. THIS IS A SAFETY VIOLATION.

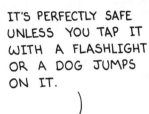
IT'S PERFECTLY SAFE UNLESS YOU TAP IT WITH A FLASHLIGHT OR A DOG JUMPS ON IT.

THIS PLAYS RIGHT INTO MY THEORY THAT CUBICLES ARE LIVING ORGANISMS.

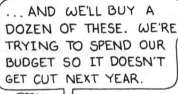
...AND WE'LL BUY A DOZEN OF THESE. WE'RE TRYING TO SPEND OUR BUDGET SO IT DOESN'T GET CUT NEXT YEAR.

THIS IS GREAT! YOU GUYS ARE SO DUMB THAT I DON'T EVEN HAVE TO USE MY FAKE PERSONALITY TO MAKE THE SALE!

...AND NINE OF THESE BLUE THINGS.

THERE'S A FULL MOON ON THE HORIZON!

SALES

ON ONE HAND, MY COMPANY DOES USE INFERIOR TECHNOLOGY IN OUR PRODUCTS...

BUT ON THE OTHER HAND, I'M THE MOST ATTRACTIVE FEMALE WHO HAS PAID ATTENTION TO YOU THIS YEAR.

WHAT KIND OF ENGINEERS DO YOU THINK WE ARE??!

DO YOU HAVE PICTURES OF YOUR FIELD SUPPORT PEOPLE?

I CAN'T BELIEVE YOU'RE RECOMMENDING THIS LOUSY VENDOR JUST BECAUSE THE SALES REP IS GORGEOUS.

HERE'S A PICTURE OF THOR, THEIR FIELD ENGINEER.

DOES HE REALLY WORK WITHOUT A SHIRT?

ONLY IF YOU BUY THE "INDIAN CHIEF" MAINTENANCE PACKAGE.

SALES

YOUR EMPLOYEES HAVE RECOMMENDED A VENDOR WHO HAS AN ATTRACTIVE SALESPERSON.

BUT THE "DOGBERT TECHNOLOGY COMPANY" CAN PROVIDE YOU WITH A HARDWARE SOLUTION FOR HALF THE COST!

I'LL SAVE MONEY!

WHAT IF I NEED TO UPGRADE LATER? IS IT EXPENSIVE?

I MUST HAVE LEFT THAT PRICE SHEET IN MY OTHER FUR.

IT'S INEXPLICABLE, BUT THE LOW-COST SYSTEM I SOLD YOU SEEMS TO BE WOEFULLY UNDER-POWERED.

YOU COULD REPLACE IT WITH ANOTHER VENDOR'S SYSTEM, THUS SHOWING EVERYBODY YOU MADE A MISTAKE. OR YOU CAN PAY MY OUTRAGEOUS UPGRADE FEES.

HOW BIG A FOOL DO YOU THINK I AM?

I WON'T KNOW UNTIL I SEE IF YOU GO FOR THE LEASE OPTION.

IT'S FUNNY — BEFORE YOUR COMPANY BOUGHT THAT CRITICAL SYSTEM FROM ME, YOU HAD ALL THE POWER...

BUT NOW, ONLY I CAN PROVIDE ESSENTIAL UPGRADES!! I CALL THE SHOTS, YOU SIMPLE FOOL!!

SEND IN THE NEXT EMPLOYEE.

AT LEAST WE DON'T HAVE ANY MULTI-VENDOR COMPATIBILITY ISSUES.

I NEED EVERYBODY TO HELP IN THE SHIPPING DEPARTMENT TODAY.

EVERY PRODUCT THAT SHIPS BEFORE THE END OF THE MONTH GETS COUNTED AS REVENUE FOR THE FISCAL YEAR. UNFORTUNATELY, WE DON'T HAVE INVENTORY.

SO WE'LL SHIP WHATEVER IS LYING AROUND, BOOK IT AS REVENUE AND SORT IT OUT LATER.

THIS ONE'S GETTING GUM.

DOGBERT MEETS WITH SOFTWARE DEVELOPERS

NOTE THE HUGE MARKET FOR SOFTWARE THAT RUNS ON THE "DOGBERT 2000" OPERATING SYSTEM.

BUT WHO CARES? THE IMPORTANT THING IS THAT I BROUGHT A BAG OF TOYS.

SOME SAY THE COMPUTER INDUSTRY IS BUILT ON SILICON. I THINK FOAM AND PLASTIC ARE EQUALLY IMPORTANT.

IN AN EFFORT TO BOOST SALES, LAPTOP COMPUTERS HAVE BEEN GIVEN TO EVERY MEMBER OF THE SALES FORCE.

THAT COULD BE A PROBLEM, GIVEN THE RECENT CUTS TO THE TRAINING BUDGET.

MEANWHILE, IN THE FIELD

AND IF YOU ORDER TODAY, I'LL THROW IN THIS RECTANGULAR PLASTIC THING.

THIS IS PHIL, RULER OF HECK, WITH A SPECIAL OFFER FOR MY PATENTED "EXERSPOON."

YOU CAN DO OVER SEVEN MILLION EXERCISES WITH THE "EXERSPOON." IT EVEN TRIMS PROBLEM AREAS!

AND THANKS TO THE INNOVATIVE SPOON SHAPE, STORAGE IS A BREEZE!

MMM...

ALTHOUGH WE ARE NOTHING BUT POND SCUM IN THIS COMPANY...

IT'S NICE TO KNOW WE CAN STILL FIND SOMEONE OF LOWER STATUS TO TORMENT.

YOU CALL THESE BROCHURES? HOW CAN I EVEN CONSIDER BUYING PRODUCTS FROM A "VEN-DUH" SUCH AS YOU?

TELL ME IF THIS HURTS.

SALES

THE CLEVER SALES-MAN EVALUATES HIS PREY.

BADGE

VISITORS SIGN IN

I HOPE HE'S AN IMPORTANT DECISION-MAKER.

TAKE ANY SEAT. I CALL THE GOOD CHAIR.

WARNING! CUBICLE! LOW-RANKING EMPLOYEE!

HERE'S OUR ORGANIZATION CHART: PRESIDENT... SENIOR VICE PRESIDENT... VICE PRESIDENT...

OKAY, LIFT YOUR FOOT. DO YOU SEE THAT COFFEE STAIN ON THE CARPET?

THAT'S YOU?

NO, THAT'S MY BOSS. I WOULD BE UNDER THE CARPET.

DO I HAVE ANY HOPE OF TALKING TO SOME-BODY WHO CAN MAKE A DECISION?

LET ME CHECK.

HEY, WALLY. WHAT'S A "DECISION"?

IT SOUNDS LIKE SOMETHING OUR COMPETITORS DO.

SOB

WHERE'S DOGBERT?

UH-OH.

ARE YOU GULLIBLE? DO YOU SPEND MONEY ON STUPID STUFF?

CALL THE "DOGBERT GULLIBLE FRIENDS HOTLINE" FOR HELP. ONLY FOUR DOLLARS PER MINUTE.

HELLO, DOGBERT. I BOUGHT AN EXERCISE MACHINE AND I'M STILL LAZY.

PLEASE HOLD.

OKAY!

CALL NOW, AND I'LL REPLACE YOUR OLD TELEVISION WITH A NEW ONE THAT LOOKS JUST LIKE IT, WHILE YOU SLEEP!

IF YOU DON'T HAVE A TOUCH TONE PHONE, STAY ON THE LINE...

UNTIL YOU GET ONE.

TORMENTING THE VENDOR

YOU MUST DO OUR BIDDING, VENDOR. WE CONTROL YOUR ECONOMIC FUTURE.

OF COURSE, OUR BUYING DECISION WILL BE BASED SOLELY ON QUANTIFIABLE PERFORMANCE MEASUREMENTS.

YOUR COMPETITOR COMPLETED THE "VENDOR CHALLENGE COURSE" IN 37 SECONDS.

AND HE GAVE US VERY NICE T-SHIRTS.

OUR NEW SLOGAN IS "EVERYBODY IS IN SALES."

IMAGINE IF ALL OUR EMPLOYEES CONVINCED THEIR FRIENDS TO BUY OUR PRODUCT, EVENTUALLY...

... WE'D HAVE NO FRIENDS?

WHAT'S THIS "FRIEND" THING I KEEP HEARING ABOUT?

SALES

MY COMPANY ASKED ALL EMPLOYEES TO ACT AS SALESPEOPLE TO FRIENDS AND FAMILY. I THINK YOU COULD USE THIS, MOM.

WHY WOULD I NEED A PRIMARY RATE CIRCUIT? I'VE ALREADY GOT A FRAME RELAY DROP TO MY WEB SERVER IN THE SEWING ROOM.

THIS IS GOING TO BE A TOUGH SALE.

HELLO-O-O! EARTH TO DILBERT! THIS IS PACKET DATA ...

DILBERT THE SALESMAN ...

YOUR COMPETITOR WAS HERE AN HOUR AGO...

HE PROMISED ME A MASSAGE FROM HELGA IF I BUY FROM HIS COMPANY. WHAT'S YOUR OFFER?

I'LL GIVE YOU MY HOUSE FOR HELGA.

YOU'RE NEW AT THIS...

SALES

Panel 1: I GOT A JOB AS A USED CAR SALESMAN.
DOES IT PAY WELL?

Panel 2: I'M NOT IN IT FOR THE MONEY. I JUST ENJOY LYING TO STRANGERS.

Panel 3: THIS ONE WAS OWNED BY CARLOS THE DIAMOND SMUGGLER. IT CORNERS WELL, BUT THE GAS MILEAGE IS BAD -- ALMOST AS IF IT HAS WEIGHTS HIDDEN IN THE DOOR PANELS.

Panel 4: DOGBERT THE CAR SALESMAN
I CAN LET YOU HAVE THIS ONE FOR FIVE THOUSAND.
THREE THOUSAND.

Panel 5: NO, BUT I COULD SELL *THAT* CAR FOR FOUR THOUSAND.
THIRTY-FIVE HUNDRED.
SOLD.

Panel 6: I GUESS YOU DON'T GET A LOT OF NEGOTIATORS LIKE ME.
IT'S THE FIRST TIME ANYBODY BOUGHT THE CAR THEY CAME HERE IN.

Panel 7: DOGBERT THE USED CAR SALESMAN
WILL THIS BE YOUR FIRST CAR, TIMMY?

Panel 8: YES, SIR... I SAVED MY MONEY FROM MOWING LAWNS.
LET'S SEE HOW MUCH YOU HAVE AND THEN I'LL PICK A CAR FOR YOU.

Panel 9: DO YOU LIKE MOWING LAWNS, TIMMY?
IT'S OKAY.
GOOD, BECAUSE I DON'T RECOMMEND MED SCHOOL FOR YOU.

Panel 10: MEETING WITH A VENDOR
I'M LARRY.

Panel 11: AND THESE PEOPLE ARE MY VAST ARRAY OF UNNECESSARY TAG-ALONGS.

Panel 12: WHAT DOES YOUR PRODUCT DO?
WE DIDN'T BRING THE GUY WHO KNOWS THAT.

SALES CONFERENCE

HERE'S THE PRODUCT YOU'LL BE SELLING NEXT QUARTER.

IT HAS NO USER INTER- FACE!

THAT MEANS NO BULKY USER MANUAL. AND NO LOSS OF FUNCTION DURING A POWER OUTAGE!

YOU WERE RIGHT. OUR SALES PEOPLE CAN'T DISTINGUISH GOOD FROM EVIL.

I STRAINED A SMILE MUSCLE.

CLAP CLAP CLAP CLAP

© 1998 United Feature Syndicate, Inc.

3/4/98

THE SALES FORCE WAS OFFERED A RETIREMENT BUYOUT PACKAGE OF FIFTY DOLLARS.

ONE HUNDRED PERCENT OF THE SALES FORCE ELECTED TO TAKE THE OFFER.

I WONDER WHAT THEY KNOW THAT I DON'T KNOW.

THERE'S A HOLE WITH NO BOTTOM.

© 1998 United Feature Syndicate, Inc.

1/2/98

WHAT ARE YOU MAKING?

COMMEMORATIVE COLLECTIBLE PLATES.

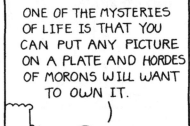

ONE OF THE MYSTERIES OF LIFE IS THAT YOU CAN PUT ANY PICTURE ON A PLATE AND HORDES OF MORONS WILL WANT TO OWN IT.

WOW! AN ACORN! AND IT'S ON A PLATE!

WHAT'S IT LIKE TO BE A MEMBER OF A HORDE?

© 1993 United Feature Syndicate, Inc.

YOU ALREADY OWN THE "ACORN SERIES" OF DOGBERT'S COMMEMORATIVE PLATES...

7-10

FOR A LIMITED TIME YOU MAY ALSO PURCHASE MY NEW ISSUE: THE "FRENCH GUY WITH A HAT" SERIES.

MY ACORN PLATES ARE MISSING.

TOMORROW I'LL INTRODUCE MY NEW SERIES: "RUSSIAN WITH FRENCH HAT."

© 1993 United Feature Syndicate, Inc.

YO, DIL-MAN!

UH-OH, IT'S KEN FROM SALES.

I TOLD OUR BIGGEST CUSTOMERS HOW GREAT OUR NEXT PRODUCT WILL BE. NOW NOBODY WILL BUY OUR CURRENT PRODUCT.

WHEN WILL THE NEW VERSION BE AVAILABLE?

IN A YEAR OR TWO.

HMM... I SEEM TO HAVE SINGLE-HANDEDLY DESTROYED AN ENTIRE PRODUCT LINE.

LUCKILY OUR BIGGEST COMPETITOR IS HIRING SALES PEOPLE. AND I'M BETTING THEY'LL HAVE BRISK SALES THIS YEAR!

COMMISSIONS GALORE!

4/21/96 © 1996 United Feature Syndicate, Inc.

IF THERE'S JUSTICE IN THIS WORLD, THE IDIOTS WILL BE PUNISHED...

...BEFORE THEY GET PROMOTED.

UM... WE NEED THE NEW VERSION BY TUESDAY.

I THOUGHT OF ANOTHER WAY TO PROFIT FROM THE IGNORANCE OF HUMANS.

I WROTE "THE DOGBERT FORMULA FOR HEALTH." I RECOMMEND A DAILY DOSE OF FOOD, SLEEP AND EXERCISE.

© 1993 United Feature Syndicate, Inc.

AND FOR ONLY $19.95 YOU CAN BUY THE PATENTED "DOGBERT JOGGEROBIC CARPET PATCH" TO HELP YOU RUN IN PLACE.

7-12

ARE YOU TIRED OF FAD DIETS AND FAD EXER-CISE DEVICES?

YES I AM!

THEN BUY MY BOOK AND GET THE REVOLUTIONARY JOGGEROBIC CARPET PATCH FOR ONLY $19.95 PLUS SHIPPING AND HANDLING.

© 1993 United Feature Syndicate, Inc.

TO PROVE IT WORKS, WE PHOTOGRAPHED AN ACTUAL ATHLETE.

PICTURES DON'T LIE!

7-13

Panel 1:
IT LOOKS LIKE SALES OF THE "DOGBERT JOGGEROBIC CARPET PATCH" ARE BRISK.

YEAH, AND I'M LOOKING TO EXPAND.

7-14

Panel 2:
RATBERT IS BUSY RESEARCHING NEW PRODUCT CONCEPTS FOR THE CARPET PATCH.

© 1993 United Feature Syndicate, Inc.

Panel 3:
"CARPET CLUB FOR MEN."

Panel 4:
DILBERT, YOU'RE BEING TEMPORARILY TRANSFERRED TO THE FIELD SALES ORGANIZATION.

© 1992 United Feature Syndicate, Inc.

Panel 5:
NORMALLY WE USE THESE ASSIGNMENTS TO ROUND SOMEBODY OUT FOR MANAGEMENT. BUT IN THIS CASE I'M JUST YANKING YOUR CHAIN!

12-14

Panel 6:
YOU'RE OVER-COMMUNICATING AGAIN, SIR.

PLUS, I HATE THE MANAGER OF SALES.

Panel 7:
SO... DILBERT, WELCOME TO THE SALES DEPARTMENT. I'M TINA, YOUR NEW BOSS.

HI

Panel 8:
AS THE NEW GUY, YOU GET THE CUSTOMERS WHO DESPISE OUR PRODUCTS AND WANT TO HURT US PERSONALLY.

12-15

Panel 9:
I HATE YOU! I HATE YOU!

YOU'LL BE SELLING TO THE SMALL BUSINESS MARKET. HE'S YOUR BEST ACCOUNT.

© 1992 United Feature Syndicate, Inc.

Panel 10:
WELCOME TO SALES TRAINING.

© 1992 United Feature Syndicate, Inc.

12-16

Panel 11:
AS YOU KNOW, OUR COMPANY MAKES OVER-PRICED, INFERIOR PRODUCTS. WE TRY TO COMPENSATE BY SETTING HIGH SALES QUOTAS.

Panel 12:
WE DON'T <u>ASK</u> YOU TO ACT ILLEGALLY, BUT IT'S PRETTY MUCH THE ONLY WAY TO REACH QUOTA. OKAY, THAT'S IT FOR TRAINING. ANY QUESTIONS?

SALES

YOUR COMPANY MAKES AN ATTRACTIVE LITTLE PRODUCT, JIM.

BUT WE'VE DECIDED TO GO WITH A VENDOR WHOSE PRODUCT ACTUALLY WORKS.

FOOLS!!! I'LL CRUSH YOU!!!

I'LL TELL YOUR BOSS YOU MADE A STUPID DECISION!! YOUR CAREERS WILL BE RUINED AND I'LL GET THE CONTRACT ANYWAY!!

YOU CAN'T SCARE US! DO YOU THINK OUR BOSS WILL BELIEVE A VENDOR OVER HIS OWN LOYAL EMPLOYEES?

MUST... KEEP... A... STRAIGHT... FACE...

HA HA HA HA HA HA HA

WE'LL TAKE A MILLION UNITS.

TAKE TWO MILLION AND I'LL SEE THAT YOU GET NICE RAISES.

I'D LIKE YOU TO MEET OUR NEWEST CUSTOMER.

YOU WON'T BE SORRY; WE'RE ONE OF THE TOP FIVE COMPANIES IN THIS FIELD.

I THOUGHT YOU SAID NO ONE ELSE MAKES THIS KIND OF PRODUCT.

NO ONE ELSE MAKES ONE WITH SO FEW FEATURES.

SO... YOUR STRATEGY IS LOW PRICE, RIGHT?

NO, HIGH MARGINS!

YOU!

I'D BETTER ASK SOMEONE WHAT A "MARGIN" IS.

... BUT BY FAR, THIS COMPUTER IS OUR MOST USER-FRIENDLY.

THE PRE-INSTALLED SOFTWARE HAS ONLY ONE BUTTON. AND WE PRESS IT BEFORE IT LEAVES THE FACTORY.

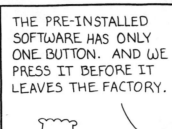

WHAT DOES IT DO?

WHOA! I'M IN OVER MY HEAD. LET ME GIVE YOU THEIR TECH SUPPORT NUMBER.

IF YOU PLAN TO REMAIN IN THE COMPUTER BUSINESS YOU'D BETTER BUNDLE THE "DOGBERT 2000" OPERATING SYSTEM WITH EVERY UNIT YOU SELL.

OTHERWISE, AFTER I DOMINATE THE MARKET YOU'LL BE LAST ON MY LIST TO RECEIVE NEW PRODUCTS!

YOU REMIND ME OF SOMEBODY...

IT'S THE GLASSES, ISN'T IT?

I'M GOING INTO THE SPORTS MEMORABILIA BUSINESS.

I'VE HEARD THAT MOST AUTOGRAPHS ARE FORGERIES, SO MY INITIAL INVESTMENT WILL BE LOW.

CAN I INTEREST YOU IN A BASEBALL SIGNED BY MOSES?

WOW! THAT'S GOING TO BE WORTH SOMETHING.

SPORTS MEMORABILIA

THIS IS THE BEST PRICE I'VE SEEN FOR A BASEBALL AUTOGRAPHED BY BABE RUTH.

BUT I DON'T SEE WHERE THE AUTOGRAPH IS.

IT GETS AUTOGRAPHED LATER TONIGHT.

I'LL TAKE THIS AND THREE OF THE HONUS WAGNER CARDS.

YOU SAY THIS FOOTBALL WAS AUTOGRAPHED BY JESUS...

BUT I'M NO FOOL. THIS ISN'T A FOOTBALL. IT HAS NO STITCHES.

THEY HEALED.

WOW!

AND I THINK I HEARD IT OINK.

AND OUR PRODUCT HAS A THIRTY TERABIT RAM CACHE, JUST LIKE YOUR COMPANY NEEDS. TELL HIM, DILBERT.

IT HAS NO RAM.

AND IT'S CAPABLE OF DETECTING TACHION FIELD EMISSIONS.

YOU'RE CONFUSING US WITH "STAR TREK" AGAIN, STAN.

WE'LL BUILD THAT STUFF INTO THE NEXT FREE UPGRADE.

WE'LL TAKE IT!

BEAM ME UP, SPOCK. THERE'S NO LIFE ON THIS PLANET.

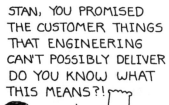

STAN, YOU PROMISED THE CUSTOMER THINGS THAT ENGINEERING CAN'T POSSIBLY DELIVER DO YOU KNOW WHAT THIS MEANS?!

IT MEANS I'M A GREAT SALESMAN AND YOU'RE A PUTRID ENGINEER.

MAYBE YOU SHOULD CONSIDER TAKING CLASSES AT NIGHT.

KARATE CLASSES

OUR DEVICE CONFORMS TO ALL INTERNATIONAL STANDARDS FOR COMMUNICATIONS.

IN OTHER WORDS, IT DOESN'T DO ANYTHING USEFUL AND IT'S NOT YOUR FAULT.

IS THERE SOMEBODY LESS EXPERIENCED I COULD TALK TO?

DO YOU HAVE MY BOSS'S NUMBER?

WAIT-A-MINUTE... I'M STARTING TO REALIZE SOMETHING.

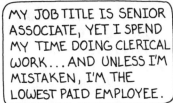

MY JOB TITLE IS SENIOR ASSOCIATE, YET I SPEND MY TIME DOING CLERICAL WORK...AND UNLESS I'M MISTAKEN, I'M THE LOWEST PAID EMPLOYEE.

IS THIS A BAD TIME?

AAAGH!! I'M A SECRETARY!

WE'RE POISED FOR SUCCESS. WE EXPECT HUGE EARNINGS AND INCREASED MARKET SHARE!

NEXT ON THE AGENDA... THERE WILL BE NO RAISES BECAUSE IT WILL BE A DIFFICULT YEAR...

CAROL, I THOUGHT I TOLD YOU TO PUT THE "UNITED WAY" UPDATE BETWEEN THOSE TWO AGENDA ITEMS.

OOPSIE.

I STAYED AWAKE FOR TWO DAYS STRAIGHT TO FINISH THIS R.F.Q. BY THE DEADLINE.

BUT IT WILL ALL BE FOR NOTHING IF YOU DON'T SEND IT OUT TODAY.

I'LL PUT IT IN THE MIDDLE OF THIS STACK SO I WON'T FORGET IT.

HERE'S MY TIME SHEET, IN EXQUISITE DETAIL.

CRINKLE CRINKLE WAD

IT'S EASIER TO INPUT THE NUMBERS IF I MAKE THEM UP AS I GO.

137

I'M COLLECTING FOR ED'S FAREWELL GIFT.

ED, YOU TREATED ME LIKE DIRT. I FIND YOU GUILTY AND I FINE YOU FIVE DOLLARS.

I JUST PUT THAT IN THERE.

COME BACK IF YOU GET MORE.

I CAN'T PROCESS YOUR VOUCHER BECAUSE THESE RECEIPTS LOOK FAKE TO ME.

THEY AREN'T FAKE!

THEN WHY AREN'T THEY NOTARIZED?

BECAUSE THEY'RE JUST RECEIPTS!

AND NOW YOU'LL TELL ME THERE'S NO DNA EVIDENCE EITHER.

HOW LONG WILL IT TAKE TO PROCESS MY VOUCHER?

I ASSIGN A PRIORITY TO EVERYONE. I'M HAPPY TO SAY YOU'RE A "ONE."

ONE CHANCE IN A MILLION.

ASK MY SECRETARY TO SCHEDULE A MEETING.

GROAN

UH...EXCUSE ME... EXCUSE ME... MISS CERBERUS, COULD A HUMBLE EMPLOYEE HAVE THE HONOR OF YOUR ATTENTION?

ARE YOU PREPARED TO TAKE THE CHALLENGE OF DEATH?!!

DOES THIS INVOLVE ANY WINGED MONKEYS?

CAROL, FROM NOW ON I'D LIKE YOU TO TYPE UP ALL OF MY INCOMING VOICE MAIL SO I CAN JUST READ IT.

AND PRINT OUT ALL OF MY E-MAIL EVERY DAY SO I DON'T HAVE TO LOG ONTO THE NETWORK.

AND GET ME A SANDWICH FROM THE CAFETERIA.

OOH, NO CASH. I'LL PAY YOU BACK.

DO YOU WANT ME TO PRECHEW THE SANDWICH OR CAN YOU HANDLE THAT ON YOUR OWN?

LISTEN UP, YOU OVERPAID ENGINEERS...

BY ORDER OF OUR RECLUSIVE BOSS, THE NEW DRESS CODE FOR ENGINEERS IS BUMBLEBEE COSTUMES.

IF YOU DON'T BELIEVE ME, SEND HIM VOICE MAIL AND ASK FOR YOURSELF.

OH, AND HE WANTS YOU TO BUY HIM A SANDWICH.

STILL NO MESSAGES THIS WEEK? IS EVERYBODY OUT SICK?

I HEARD THEY HAVE HIVES.

CAROL, IF YOU HAVE ANY SUGGESTIONS ON MY REPORT, LET ME KNOW.

WHAT KIND OF RIDICULOUS TRIPE ARE YOU PUSHING??

I SPIT ON YOUR REPORT!

PTOO! PTOO!

I SHOULD BURN IT TO ASHES, BUT I WON'T...

BECAUSE I'D RATHER DANCE ON YOUR GRAVE AFTER PEOPLE READ THIS! HA HA HA HA!

CRAWL BACK INTO YOUR HOLE, YOU FLY-INFESTED BUCKET OF DEAD CARP!!

PTOINK

DIE! DIE! DIE!

NEXT TIME I'M JUST GONNA SAY "CAROL, MAKE SOME COPIES."

THE SECRETARIES HERE HAVE WAY TOO MUCH POWER.

DILBERT *Gives You the Business*

SECRETARIES

CAROL, ABOUT THIS FLIGHT TO NEW YORK THAT YOU BOOKED FOR ME...

IS IT REALLY NECESSARY TO MAKE ALL THESE STOPOVERS IN THIRD-WORLD COUNTRIES THAT ARE EXPERIENCING REBEL INSURRECTIONS?

YOU'D BETTER WEAR THE INTERNATIONAL SYMBOL OF THE "RED CROSS" ON YOUR BACK.

HERE'S MY TIME SHEET, FILLED OUT IN INCREMENTS OF FIFTEEN MINUTES.

AS USUAL, I CODED THE USELESS HOURS SPENT IN MEETINGS AS "WORK," WHEREAS THE TIME I SPENT IN THE SHOWER DESIGNING CIRCUITS IN MY MIND IS "NON-WORK."

INTERESTINGLY, EVEN THE TIME I SPEND COMPLAIN-ING ABOUT MY LACK OF PRODUCTIVITY IS CONSIDERED "WORK."

I HATE MY LIFE.

SEND THIS BY E-MAIL.

FAX IT, TOO, IN CASE HE DOESN'T CHECK HIS E-MAIL. AND MAIL THE ORIGINAL SO HE HAS A CLEAN COPY.

GOODBYE "PAPERLESS," HELLO "CLUELESS."

OH MY! THIS IS SHOCKING!

WHAT?

40% OF ALL SICK DAYS TAKEN BY YOUR STAFF ARE FRIDAYS AND MONDAYS!

WHAT KIND OF IDIOT DO THEY THINK I AM?

NOT AN IDIOT SAVANT. THEY CAN DO MATH.

BASED ON A TRUE STORY

I'M DROWNING IN WORK!

YOU HAVE TO DO SOMETHING.

I COULD BUILD A PARTITION RIGHT HERE.

HOW WILL A PARTITION HELP?

CAROL, YOU SHOULDN'T BE AFRAID TO TRY NEW THINGS.

IF IT DOESN'T WORK, WE'LL TRY SOMETHING ELSE!

ARE YOU OVER THERE? IT WORKS!

HERE'S MY TIME SHEET, INCLUDING GUESSES FOR THE NEXT TWO DAYS SO I CAN MEET YOUR ARBITRARY CLERICAL DEADLINE.

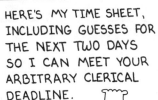

IF ANYTHING IMPORTANT COMES UP, I'LL IGNORE IT TO PRESERVE THE INTEGRITY OF THE TIME-REPORTING SYSTEM.

ARE YOU FINISHED ANNOYING ME YET? ACCORDING TO MY TIME SHEET I'LL BE HERE FOR ANOTHER 14 MINUTES.

CAROL, I ASKED YOU TO ENROLL ME IN THE QUALITY COLLEGE, BUT THE CONFIRMATION SAYS CLOWN COLLEGE.

IT'S A PREREQUISITE COURSE.

THIS IS GONNA COST ME ON SECRETARIES DAY. I HOPE IT'S OKAY TO BE AN ANGRY CLOWN.

SECRETARIES

MAY I SLIP IN? I ONLY NEED ONE COPY.

WHAT'S THE MESSAGE HERE? IS _YOUR_ TIME WORTH MORE THAN _MY_ TIME BECAUSE YOU'RE A MANAGER AND I'M A SECRETARY? HUH?

THIS MIGHT STING FOR A SECOND, BUT IT'LL REMOVE YOUR DESIRE TO MAKE COPIES.

THE "SECRETARY WITH A CROSSBOW" GOES ON THE HUNT.

MOBY DICK!

YOU'VE BEEN HARPOONED AGAIN, SIR.

YEAH, BUT I CAPSIZED HER DESK.

IT MUST BE GREAT TO BE A SECURITY GUARD.

YOU HAVE THE ENTIRE DAY TO LET YOUR MIND TRANSPORT YOU TO MAGIC REALMS OF WONDER AND CREATIVITY.

I WONDER WHAT BALSA WOOD TASTES LIKE.

ALICE, YOU'VE GOT TO LOCK UP THESE PROPRIETARY DOCUMENTS YOU HAVE IN YOUR CUBICLE.

IF OUR COMPETITORS SEE OUR PLANS, IT COULD BE VERY DANGEROUS.

FOR US OR FOR THEM?

THE COMPETITORS

OOH! LOOK! THEY'RE PLANNING TO "UTILIZE SYNERGY." WE'RE IN TROUBLE NOW!

HA HA HA HA

STOP! YOU'RE KILLING ME!!

HI, TIM. WHAT ARE YOU WORKING ON THESE DAYS?

A SECRET PROJECT.

VERY, VERY SECRET. CONFIDENTIAL AND PROPRIETARY. REAL HUSH-HUSH.

IT SOUNDS IMPORTANT.

JUST MOVE ALONG.

HALT AND SUBMIT TO THE MIND SCAN OF "BRAINITOR, THE GUARDIAN OF SECURITY."

THE BAG CONTAINS ONE COMPUTER..."PENTIUM" PROCESSOR... ONE GIG HARD DRIVE...HIGHLY FRAGMENTED...

PLEASE WAIT WHILE I OPTIMIZE YOUR HARD DISK...

THIS IS VAGUELY UNSETTLING.

I'M PUTTING YOU ON THE STRATEGIC PLANNING TEAM.

IT'S LIKE WORK BUT WITHOUT THE SATISFACTION OF ACCOMPLISHING ANYTHING.

YOU'RE NEW, SO LET ME EXPLAIN HOW THIS WORKS.

WE HAVE MEETINGS AND TALK ABOUT THE COMPANY'S STRATEGY IN VAGUE EMOTIONAL TERMS.

IN TIME, WE CONVINCE OURSELVES THAT WE'RE MORE THAN MEDIOCRE THINKERS WHO SIT AROUND COMPLAINING.

WE START BELIEVING OUR OPINIONS WILL STEER THE COMPANY. WE FEEL IMPORTANT. WE FEEL **ALIVE**!!

THEN WE SNAP OUT OF IT AND MAKE VIEWGRAPHS THAT SAY WE SHOULD KEEP DOING WHAT WE'RE DOING.

I LIKE MAKING VIEWGRAPHS.

ACTUALLY, WE USE LAST YEAR'S VIEWGRAPH

STRATEGY AND PLANNING

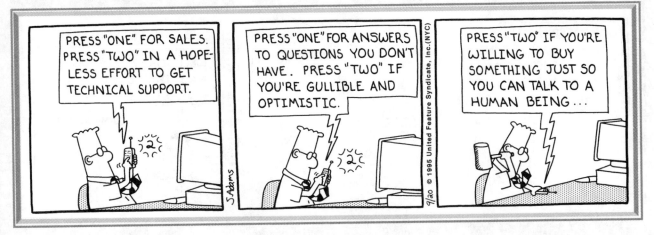

HELLO, IS THIS THE "HELP DESK"?

NO, THAT GROUP GOT REENGINEERED OUT OF EXISTENCE.

I'M THE NEW "NO HELP WHATSOEVER DESK." MY JOB IS TO MAKE SURE YOU NEVER CALL AGAIN.

CAN YOU TELL ME HOW TO MAKE A PIE CHART?

CRUSH YOUR COMPUTER INTO SMALL CHUNKS, ADD FLOUR AND BAKE ONE HOUR.

WHILE YOU'RE WAITING, READ THE FREE NOVEL WE SENT YOU. IT'S A SPANISH STORY ABOUT A GUY NAMED "MANUAL."

REPEAT THE PROCESS UNTIL YOU GET THE DESIRED RESULT.

THIS LOST A LOT IN THE TRANSLATION.

WE'RE DISCONTINUING TECHNICAL SUPPORT OF ALL OUR PRODUCTS.

A RECORDED MESSAGE WILL EXPLAIN IT TO THE CALLER THIS WAY...

"IN ORDER TO SERVE CUSTOMERS BETTER, WE'VE DISCONTINUED TECHNICAL SUPPORT."

HOW DOES THAT SERVE CUSTOMERS BETTER?

WE'LL REDIRECT THOSE RESOURCES TO OTHER AREAS.

WHAT OTHER AREAS?

PROFITS.

THAT MAKES YOUR BONUS LARGER.

ANY OTHER QUESTIONS?

APPARENTLY I'M ENGULFED IN EVIL.

THAT'S THE SPIRIT!

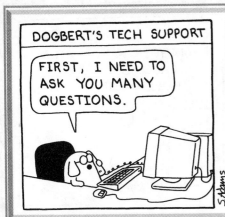

DOGBERT'S TECH SUPPORT

FIRST, I NEED TO ASK YOU MANY QUESTIONS.

THEN I WILL TRANSFER YOU TO SOMEONE WHO WILL ASK THE SAME QUESTIONS AGAIN.

WE DO THIS TO REMOVE ANY HOPE YOU MIGHT HAVE HAD THAT WE UNDERSTAND TECHNOLOGY.

DOGBERT'S TECH SUPPORT

I THINK I KNOW WHAT YOUR PROBLEM IS...

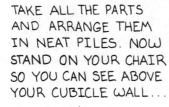

TAKE ALL THE PARTS AND ARRANGE THEM IN NEAT PILES. NOW STAND ON YOUR CHAIR SO YOU CAN SEE ABOVE YOUR CUBICLE WALL...

NOW SHOUT "DOES ANY-BODY KNOW HOW TO READ A MANUAL?"

DOGBERT'S TECH SUPPORT

THIS IS DOGBERT. HOW MAY I ABUSE YOU?

I NEED TO MOVE MY CURSOR TO THE RIGHT BUT MY MOUSE IS AT THE EDGE OF THE MOUSEPAD.

HAVE YOU TRIED REBOOTING WITHOUT SAVING YOUR FILES?

YEAH, SEVERAL TIMES.

HAVE YOU TRIED MOVING YOUR DESK?

IT DIDN'T WORK.

YOU NEED MY $800 MOUSEPAD UPGRADE.

WHAT ACCOUNT DOES THIS GET CHARGED TO?

"IDIOT EXPENSE," JUST LIKE EVERY-THING ELSE.

DOGBERT'S TECH SUPPORT

ACCORDING TO MY ONLINE DATABASE, OUR PRODUCT ISN'T COMPATIBLE WITH YOUR COMPUTER.

IT'S ALSO INCOMPATIBLE WITH ALL OTHER COMPUTERS AND ALL OTHER SOFTWARE INCLUDING OUR OWN.

AND THOSE RED BLOTCHES ON YOUR HANDS — THAT'S BECAUSE OUR BOX IS MADE OF POISON IVY.

DOGBERT'S TECH SUPPORT

PLEASE WAIT WHILE I CONSULT WITH SOMEBODY WHO HAS YOUR EXACT SAME PROBLEM.

HOW DO YOU COMPENSATE FOR A TINY BRAIN, RATBERT?

I JUST SAY I'M WAY TOO BUSY TO LEARN. THEN I GET SOMEBODY ELSE TO DO MY WORK.

I'M GOING TO TRANSFER YOU TO AN EXPERT.

SOMETIMES I PRETEND TO BE DEAD.

OUR NEW STRATEGY IS TO MAKE DEFECTIVE PRODUCTS AND CHARGE FOR TECHNICAL SUPPORT.

HEH-HEH... OUR USER MANUAL IS TOTALLY INCOMPREHENSIBLE. WE DIDN'T PLAN IT THAT WAY — WE WERE LUCKY.

I'M SO PROUD TO BE HERE.

IT ALL CAME TOGETHER WHEN I REALIZED I HATE OUR CUSTOMERS.

TINA, YOU'LL HAVE TO HAVE ALL THE DOCUMENTATION WRITTEN BY NEXT WEEK SO WE CAN SHIP IT WHEN THE SOFTWARE IS DONE.

HOW CAN I WRITE INSTRUCTIONS FOR SOMETHING THAT DOESN'T EXIST YET?

YOU'LL HAVE TO MAKE LOGICAL GUESSES.

"IF YOU PRESS ANY KEY YOUR COMPUTER WILL LOCK UP. IF YOU CALL OUR TECH SUPPORT WE'LL BLAME 'MICROSOFT.'"

I WANT YOU THREE TO WRITE THE DEPARTMENT NEWSLETTER. IT'S AN IMPORTANT, HIGH-PROFILE ASSIGNMENT.

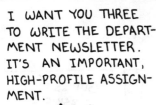

I AM AN EXPERIENCED TECHNICAL WRITER. YOU HAVE PLACED ME ON A PROJECT WITH AN INTERN AND A RODENT.

MY NEXT RAISE WILL DEPEND ON THEIR PERFORMANCE.

I'LL DO THE SPORTS PAGE!

I'LL BE THE TOPLESS MODEL ON PAGE TWO.

LET'S GET ONE THING STRAIGHT BEFORE WE START WRITING THE DEPARTMENT NEWSLETTER...

I'M AN EXPERIENCED TECHNICAL WRITER. YOU ARE AN INTERN AND A RAT, RESPECTIVELY. THEREFORE I WILL BE THE EDITOR.

I HAVE NO SKILLS WHATSOEVER. THEREFORE I'LL BE EXECUTIVE EDITOR.

IS "PUBLISHER" TAKEN?

AT THE RISK OF DYING FROM BOREDOM, I MUST INTERVIEW YOU FOR THE DEPARTMENT NEWSLETTER.

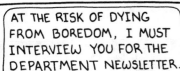

LET ME GIVE YOU SOME BACKGROUND BEFORE I TALK ABOUT MY PROJECT...

"THE PROJECT IS GOOD," QUIPPED THE ENGINEER.

...SO THERE I AM IN MY MOM'S FALLOPIAN TUBE...

WALLY, I'M HOPING YOU'LL AGREE TO WRITE ABOUT YOUR PROJECT FOR THE NEWSLETTER...

AND IN THE GRAND TRADITION OF ENGINEERING, I EXPECT YOU'LL GIVE THIS THE LOWEST PRIORITY, THUS MAKING ME DESPISE YOU.

SO... ARE YOU SAYING YOU DON'T DESPISE ME NOW?

WE ARE NOT HAVING A "MOMENT" HERE!

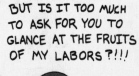

DOGBERT, CAREER COUNSELOR

I'M A LOWLY TECHNICAL WRITER NOW, BUT MY GOAL IS TO BECOME A FAMOUS NOVELIST.

MY PLAN IS TO WRITE WITTY AND SCATHING E-MAIL MESSAGES ABOUT CO-WORKERS UNTIL A PUBLISHER GIVES ME AN ADVANCE.

THEY MIGHT EXPECT YOU TO WRITE A BOOK AT SOME POINT.

BLOOD SUCKERS!

WALLY, DID YOU REVIEW MY DRAFT OF THE USER MANUAL YET?

THE CHARACTERS IN THE EXAMPLES GAVE ME NO REASON TO CARE ABOUT THEM. IT LEFT ME EMPTY.

SADLY, USER "B" COULD NEVER LOVE USER "A" BECAUSE HE WAS A BALD ENGINEER.

DOGBERT TWEAKS TINA THE BRITTLE TECH WRITER

IS TECHNICAL WRITING THE SAME AS WORD PROCESSING?

NO!!!

I AM A HIGHLY SKILLED COMMUNICATIONS PROFESSIONAL! I CAN TAKE JUMBLES OF INERT THOUGHTS AND BRING THEM TO LIFE!!

MY SECRETARY IS RUNNING THE STAFF MEETING. I NEED YOU TO RETYPE THIS ORG CHART.

THE DOCTOR IS IN!

TO: ALL ENGINEERS
FROM: TINA THE TECH WRITER

GIVE ME THE INFORMATION I REQUESTED, OR SOW THE SEEDS OF YOUR OWN DESTRUCTION!

ONE SHOULD NEVER COMPOSE E-MAIL WHILE ONE IS SNARLING.

I'M CREATING A DIGITAL ARCHIVE OF THE WORLD'S GREATEST ART. BUT MY BOSS INSISTS ON "FIXING" THE ARTISTS' MISTAKES.

HEE HEE

THIS IS SUCH A FUNNY STORY FOR THE NEWSLETTER!

IT'S A FUNNY STORY, BUT CHANGE "FIXING" TO "DRAMATICALLY IMPROVING."

I SHOULD QUIT AND BECOME A CONTRACT EMPLOYEE. THEN I'D HAVE MORE INCOME AND I'D FEEL THE WIND IN MY HAIR.

IT'S POSSIBLE YOU'D HAVE NO INCOME AT ALL...

AND IF YOU WANT WIND IN YOUR HAIR YOU'LL HAVE TO TAKE OFF YOUR SHIRT AND RUN AROUND WITH YOUR ARMS UP.

THANK YOU FOR YOUR SUPPORT.

ALICE, I'M THINKING ABOUT QUITTING AND BECOMING A CONTRACT EMPLOYEE. DO YOU HAVE ANY ADVICE?

SLEEP IN DOORWAYS SO IT DOESN'T RAIN ON YOU. THE BEST SHOPPING CARTS ARE AT "LUCKY." YOU CAN MAKE AN EXCELLENT SIGN WITH A BLACK MARKING PEN AND A HUNK OF CARDBOARD.

I HATE ALL OF MY CO-WORKERS.

DESPITE THE NAME, FOOD STAMPS ARE NOT EDIBLE.

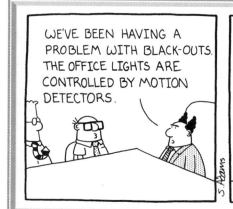

WE'VE BEEN HAVING A PROBLEM WITH BLACK-OUTS. THE OFFICE LIGHTS ARE CONTROLLED BY MOTION DETECTORS.

I HIRED A TEMP TO WALK AROUND AND FLAP HIS ARMS SO THE LIGHTS WON'T GO OFF.

ANOTHER JOURNALISM MAJOR ENTERS THE WORKFORCE.

IT SEEMS LIKE A WASTE. MAYBE HE COULD FAN US.

TEMPS AND CONTRACT EMPLOYEES

I JUST LOVE HIRING THESE TEMPORARY WORKERS!

NO EMPLOYEE BENE-FITS... NO UNION... JUST TOSS 'EM IN THE DUMPSTER WHEN YOU'RE DONE WITH THEM!

THE DUMPSTER SEEMS A BIT INAPPROPRIATE.

THEY'RE WAY TOO BIG TO FLUSH.

WOW! YOU TEMPO-RARY CONTRACT PROGRAMMERS SURE ARE PRODUCTIVE!

IT MUST BE EXCITING TO KNOW YOU CAN BE DISMISSED AT ANY MOMENT. YOUR VERY SURVIVAL DEPENDS ON RESULTS!

LET'S GO BLAME MARKETING FOR NOT GIVING US DETAILED REQUIRE-MENTS.

WHAT'S THE BIG RUSH?

WE'RE PLANNING TO HIRE A TEMP AT WORK. YOU SHOULD APPLY FOR THE JOB, RATBERT.

WOW! ME? A TEMP?!

AS A TEMP I WOULD FINALLY GET ALL OF THE RESPECT AND UNCONDITIONAL LOVE THAT I DESERVE!!

DANGER: SHARP LEARNING CURVE AHEAD.

I ASSUME I'LL GET AN OFFICE AND A SECRETARY.

I SUBMIT MYSELF AS A CANDIDATE FOR THE POSITION OF "TEMPORARY EMPLOYEE."

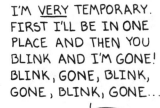

I'M VERY TEMPORARY. FIRST I'LL BE IN ONE PLACE AND THEN YOU BLINK AND I'M GONE! BLINK, GONE, BLINK, GONE, BLINK, GONE...

STOP SAYING "BLINK, GONE." IT'S MAKING ME NUTS.

IT APPEARS THAT THE BALANCE OF POWER HAS SHIFTED MY WAY.

CATBERT: EVIL H.R. DIRECTOR

YES, REGULAR EMPLOYEES ARE PAID LESS THAN CONTRACT EMPLOYEES SUCH AS YOURSELF.

BUT IF YOU JOIN THE COMPANY, YOU'LL GET MANY INTANGIBLE BENEFITS.

MAYBE YOUR STOCK-HOLDERS WOULD LIKE SOME INTANGIBLE BENEFITS. THEY CAN HAVE MINE.

© 1998 United Feature Syndicate, Inc.

WE JUST SHIPPED OUR NEWEST PRODUCT. YOU FOLKS IN TECH SUPPORT WILL NEED TO BE TRAINED SO YOU CAN AVOID ANY EMBARRASSMENTS.

WE HAD A MONK WRITE THE TRAINING MATERIAL ON A GRAIN OF RICE. WE COULD ONLY AFFORD ONE, SO YOU'LL HAVE TO SHARE IT.

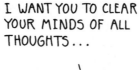

© 1995 United Feature Syndicate, Inc. (NYC)

TO BE HONEST, I'M NOT SURE WE HAD A REAL MONK. HE WROTE EVERY-THING IN PIG LATIN.

SECOND DAY: DOGBERT'S SCHOOL FOR SELF-SERVICE GAS STATION ATTENDANTS

YOU MUST LEARN TO RELAX...

I WANT YOU TO CLEAR YOUR MINDS OF ALL THOUGHTS...

THAT WAS TOO EASY.

© 1991 United Feature Syndicate, Inc.

I'M GOING TO OPEN A SCHOOL FOR PEOPLE WITH NO COMMON SENSE.

WHO WOULD PAY TO GO TO A SCHOOL THAT TEACHES SOMETHING THAT CAN'T BE LEARNED?

© 1992 United Feature Syndicate, Inc.

EXCEPT MAYBE PEOPLE WITH NO COMMON SENSE...

BINGO.

WELCOME TO DOGBERT'S SCHOOL OF COMMON SENSE.

I'VE ASKED YOU TO PAY TUITION IN ADVANCE; THAT WAY IF YOU'RE UNSATISFIED WITH THE SCHOOL, YOU'LL HAVE THE ADDED NEGOTIATING LEVERAGE OF HAVING ALREADY PAID.

AND THANKS, ALICE, FOR ASKING IF TIPPING IS CUSTOMARY.

I'M GOING TO OPEN A SCHOOL FOR PEOPLE WHO ARE TECHNOLOGY IMBECILES.

I'LL TEACH PEOPLE HOW TO USE AUTOMATIC BANK MACHINES, MICROWAVE OVENS, VIDEO RECORDERS, CD PLAYERS, THAT *SORT* OF THING...

I THOUGHT HE WAS REASONABLY BRIGHT UNTIL WE GOT THE VCR...

THEY CAN FOOL YOU.

Imbecile Admissions

WELCOME TO DOGBERT'S SCHOOL FOR TECHNOLOGY IMBECILES.

YOU ARE ALL EASILY BAFFLED BY SIMPLE TECHNOLOGY, EVEN THOUGH YOU HAVE NORMAL INTELLIGENCE OTHERWISE.

OF COURSE, I'M GENERALIZING ON THAT LAST POINT.

BEER!

DOGBERT'S SCHOOL FOR TECHNOLOGY IMBECILES

CAN ANYBODY SHOW ME WHAT YOU DO WITH A MICRO-WAVE?

I INSERT THE VIDEO TAPE... THEN I SET THE TIMER FOR NINETY MINUTES...

DOES ANYBODY KNOW WHY IT ISN'T WORKING?

THE FOOL! IT'S BETA!

LET'S GO AROUND THE CIRCLE AND SHARE WHAT WE LEARNED IN THE THREE-DAY WORKSHOP.

TEAM

AT FIRST I THOUGHT IT WAS A WASTE OF OUR TRAINING BUDGET...

THEN YOU ASKED US TO FORM TEAMS AND MAKE PAPER AIRPLANES WHILE BLINDFOLDED...

I DON'T KNOW IF IT WAS BECAUSE OF THE DARKNESS OR THE WAY WE SHARED OUR THOUGHTS ABOUT FLIGHT...

BUT SUDDENLY I FOUND UNCONDITIONAL LOVE FOR MY CO-WORKERS.

BE THEY ACCOUNTANTS, BE THEY MARKETEERS OR BE THEY SECRETARIES.

AS A RESULT, I'VE BECOME A COMPETITIVE LION, EAGER TO POUNCE ON MY WORKLOAD AND INCREASE STOCK-HOLDER VALUES!!

THANK YOU, WALLY.

DILBERT, WHAT DID YOU LEARN?

I LEARNED THAT YOU SHOULDN'T PUT A LITTLE ERASER-PILOT IN YOUR PAPER AIRPLANE.

SOMEBODY NEEDS A GROUP HUG!

TRAINING

WELCOME TO DOGBERT'S "SCHOOL OF HARD KNOCKS."

THIS IS THE SCHOOL YOU'VE HEARD SO MUCH ABOUT.

CHANCES ARE, ONE OF YOUR PARENTS IS A GRADUATE OF THIS SCHOOL.

AT DOGBERT'S SCHOOL OF HARD KNOCKS, YOU WILL GAIN THE WISDOM THAT CAN ONLY BE OBTAINED THROUGH SUFFERING.

THROUGHOUT THE COURSE, I'LL BE WHACKING YOU WITH VARIOUS BLUNT OBJECTS.

IT MAY BE UNPLEASANT AT FIRST, BUT YOU'LL GET USED TO IT.

EVENTUALLY, YOUR BRAIN WILL RATIONALIZE THE WHOLE EXPERIENCE. YOU'LL THINK I'M A DEDICATED TEACHER, AND YOU'LL ACTUALLY BELIEVE YOU LEARNED SOMETHING.

STICK WITH THE BASICS, I SAY.

5-26

JOB IMPEDIMENTS

ANNOYING
CO-WORKERS

GEE, TIM, YOU LOOK AWFUL.

I'VE BEEN WORKING FOR FIVE DAYS WITHOUT ANY SLEEP TO FINISH THIS REPORT.

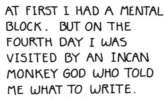

AT FIRST I HAD A MENTAL BLOCK. BUT ON THE FOURTH DAY I WAS VISITED BY AN INCAN MONKEY GOD WHO TOLD ME WHAT TO WRITE.

WOW, LUCKY BREAK.

NOW I JUST HAVE TO FIND SOMEBODY WHO CAN TRANSLATE HIS SIMPLE BUT BEAUTIFUL LANGUAGE.

UH-OH, NARDO IS COMING. I'M OUT OF HERE.

UH, HI, NARDO.

IN THE OLD COUNTRY WE DID NOT HAVE WHAT YOU CALL PERSONAL SPACE.

TAKE YOUR HANDS OUT OF MY POCKETS.

OH, I GET IT. THEY'RE FOR YOUR USE ONLY, RIGHT?

DILBERT, THIS IS YOUR NEW CO-WORKER, FLOYD REMORA.

FLOYD HAS WORKED HERE FOR TWENTY YEARS WITHOUT DEVELOPING ANY SKILLS. HE SURVIVES BY ATTACHING HIMSELF TO THE BACKS OF OTHER EMPLOYEES.

GO AHEAD... ASK ME HOW MY DAY WENT.

I SEE IT'S YOUR TURN TO WORK WITH FLOYD.

YEAH.

HE LIVED ON MY BACK FOR A YEAR, SHARING MY SUCCESSES WITHOUT CONTRIBUTING.

I HAD HIM LANCED.

DOES IT LEAVE A BIG HICKEY?

ANNOYING CO-WORKERS

IT'S NOT MY POLICY TO FIRE MORONS, DONALD. FIRING IS EXPENSIVE.

IT'S MY POLICY TO MAKE YOUR JOB SO UNPLEASANT THAT YOU QUIT.

SO, YOUR PROJECT INVOLVES BEING BITTEN BY COYOTES?

ONLY TWO MORE YEARS AND I'M VESTED.

I HAVE NO USEFUL SKILLS OR KNOWLEDGE. I COMPENSATE BY "RAISING ISSUES."

OUR SALESPEOPLE HAVEN'T BEEN TRAINED FOR THE NEW PRODUCT!!

SOMEONE SHOULD HAVE A MEETING ABOUT THAT.

WOW, I CAN ACTUALLY HEAR OXYGEN BEING WASTED.

I'M A WORTHLESS EMPLOYEE WHO CUTS OUT NEWSPAPER ARTICLES AND ROUTES THEM AROUND.

I USED TO MAKE SURE THE ARTICLES WERE RELEVANT, BUT THAT WAS MORE WORK THAN IT WAS WORTH.

I SAW THIS ALREADY.

IT'S FROM YOUR PAPER. YOU ALWAYS LEAVE IT IN THE THIRD STALL.

EXCUSE ME. I COULDN'T AVOID HEARING YOUR CONVERSATION OUTSIDE MY CUBICLE.

I THINK I SPEAK FOR A LOT OF CUBICLE DWELLERS WHEN I SAY...

SHUT UP!!

ARE YOU THE POMPOUS AIRBAG OF THE OFFICE?

INDEED.

I'VE BEEN ASKED TO DEFLATE YOU.

MY SOURCES TELL ME THAT YOU COMBINE ARROGANCE WITH TRIVIA AND TRY TO PASS IT OFF AS INTELLIGENCE.

THAT'S BECAUSE I'M SURROUNDED BY FOOLS WHO DON'T EVEN KNOW THE CAPITAL OF ELBONIA!

I HAVE A SIGNED STATEMENT FROM YOUR WIFE...

...THAT YOU PUT WET LAUNDRY IN THE OVEN LAST NIGHT.

THAT EXPLAINS THE CHEWY CASSEROLE SHE SERVED ME THIS MORNING.

DOGBERT'S FIRST LAW OF BUSINESS

REALITY IS ALWAYS CONTROLLED BY THE PEOPLE WHO ARE MOST INSANE.

EXAMPLE

THANKS FOR AGREEING TO WORK ON MY PROJECT.

I NEVER AGREED TO WORK ON YOUR PROJECT.

YOU CAN'T CHANGE YOUR MIND NOW! IT'S TOO LATE TO GET SOMEONE ELSE!

UM... I'M NOT CHANGING MY MIND. I CLEARLY SAID I WOULD NOT WORK ON YOUR PROJECT.

YOU LYING WEASEL! I'LL RUIN YOU!!

OKAY! OKAY! I'LL WORK ON YOUR PROJECT!

WALLY, THANKS FOR AGREEING TO DONATE YOUR COMPUTER TO MY PROJECT.

WHAT?

ANNOYING CO-WORKERS

I JUST GAVE MY TWO-WEEK NOTICE.

YES! YES! THE ARROGANT, OBSTRUCTIONIST BORE IS HISTORY!

EVERYONE SEEMS TO BE TAKING THIS RATHER WELL.

COUNT ME IN FOR THE GOODBYE LUNCH!

OKAY, THE STAFF MEETING IS OVER. DOES ANYBODY HAVE ANY MEANINGLESS, RAMBLING QUESTIONS?

JOHNSON?

HOW CAN WE WORK AS A TEAM TO ACHIEVE TOTAL QUALITY WITHOUT SACRIFICING CUSTOMER FOCUS?

HOW MANY PEOPLE WOULD LIKE TO SEE ME MAKE JOHNSON FETCH THIS STICK?

IF THERE ARE NO OBJECTIONS, I'D LIKE TO MAKE FUNNY FACES AND TELL A LONG RAMBLING STORY.

... SO, THEN I SAID "YOU WANT THE <u>MONTHLY</u> REPORT, NOT THE <u>DAILY</u> REPORT."... BUT THAT GOT ME THINKING... SO...

BLAH BLAH BLAH

I CAN TOP THAT.

I NEED THIS INFORMATION TODAY. PLUS A COMPLETE ANALYSIS OF THE ALTERNATIVES.

CRINKLE CRINKLE STUFF

THAT WASN'T NICE.

IN TODAY'S LESSON, YOU LEARN THAT YOU'RE MY CO-WORKER, NOT MY BOSS.

WALLY, I NEED YOUR INPUT ON THIS BY THE END OF THE DAY.

PLEASE DROP YOUR REQUEST HERE, IN "WALLY'S PILE OF PERPETUAL IGNORAGE."

CAN'T I JUST GIVE IT TO YOU?

I DON'T LIKE TO TOUCH THAT STUFF WITH MY HANDS.

IT'S TIME FOR A VISIT FROM "CAMPING CARL."

THERE GOES MY ENTIRE MORNING.

I'D LIKE TO BEGIN WITH A MONOLOGUE ENTITLED "WOE IS CARL."

I'M WORKING EVERY MINUTE!

THEY ALL LAUGHED WHEN I BUILT THE ESCAPE TUNNEL.

MY WIFE SEWS ALL OF MY WORK CLOTHES. SHE'S THE TALENTED ONE IN THE FAMILY.

SHE HATES YOU, DOESN'T SHE?

WHY DO YOU ASK?

IF I DON'T ACCEPT THE TRANSFER TO A FROZEN ASTEROID, I'LL BE SURPLUSSED.

TED, LET ME SHOW YOU SOMETHING ON THIS MAP.

SEE THIS TINY ISLAND?

YES.

THAT'S WHERE THE PEOPLE WHO CARE LIVE.

DILBERT *Gives You the Business*

BUSINESS LANGUAGE

172

DILBERT *Gives You the Business*

BUSINESS LANGUAGE

MY ACCOMPLISHMENT THIS WEEK IS THAT I'VE BECOME AN AGENT OF CHANGE.

I FOSTER AND REWARD THOSE BEHAVIORS THAT CONTRIBUTE TO A CULTURE OF TEAMWORK.

I'VE BECOME SLIGHTLY MORE CYNICAL.

KEEP UP THE GOOD WORK, BUDDY.

PAT PAT

I GOT A BROCHURE FOR "DOGBERT'S SEMINAR ON MANAGEMENT ZOMBIES." I THINK YOU SHOULD GO.

"LEARN HOW TO USE WORDS LIKE: UTILIZE, PARADIGM, VERTICAL EMPOWERMENT, AND PROACTIVE IN EVERY SENTENCE."

I'M NOT SURE I WANT TO TALK LIKE THAT.

COME... JOIN US... DON'T BE AFRAID...

MANY OF YOU COME TO MY MANAGEMENT SEMINAR AS OPTIMISTIC, CREATIVE, CLEAR-SPEAKING INDIVIDUALS.

BUT WITH HARD WORK, YOU CAN BECOME JARGON-SPEWING CORPORATE ZOMBIES, LIKE CARL HERE.

I WANT TO DIALOGUE WITH YOU ABOUT UTILIZING RESOURCES.

GOOD BOY! HERE'S A DONUT.

DOGBERT'S SEMINAR ON MANAGEMENT ZOMBIES

AS A ZOMBIE, YOU MUST SPEAK IN EMPTY GENERAL-ITIES.

YOUR BUSINESS PLAN MIGHT SAY "WE STRIVE TO UTILIZE A VARIETY OF TECHNIQUES TO ACCOMPLISH A BROAD SPECTRUM OF RESULTS TOWARD THE BOTTOM LINE."

HEY! MY SKIN IS GETTING CLAMMY AND I HAVE THE URGE TO CALL A MEETING!

ME TOO!

GOOD... GOOD...

BUSINESS LANGUAGE EXPLAINED

NICE BARREL.

THIS OLD THING?

MEANING: SAY GOODBYE TO SALARY INCREASES.

HELLO.

MEANING: WE CAN'T FIND OUR BUTTS WITH BOTH HANDS.

I PROCLAIM THIS TO BE "GREEN INK DAY."

MEANING: YOU'RE THE MONARCH OF UNIMPORTANT DECISIONS.

"WE'RE REENGINEERING YOUR FUNCTION."

MEANING: ADIOS, TONTO, AND THE HORSE YOU RODE IN ON.

YOU WERE A CANNIBAL?

I'M A PEOPLE PERSON.

MEANING: WE'RE TRYING TO HIRE SOME TRAINED PEOPLE.

WHAT'S YOUR FAVORITE ODOR?

RESEARCH

MEANING: WE BLAME CUSTOMERS FOR OUR LACK OF INNOVATION.

THANKS FOR LISTENING.

HA HA HA!

MEANING: WE THINK HUMOR IS IMPORTANT.

I WANT YOU TO INTERVIEW THE NEW CANDIDATE FOR ENGINEERING. DON'T REVEAL ANY UGLY TRUTHS.

AT THIS COMPANY WE'RE DEDICATED TO THE PRINCIPLE OF EMPLOYEE EMPOWERMENT, JENNIFER.

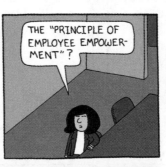

THE "PRINCIPLE OF EMPLOYEE EMPOWERMENT"?

UH-OH.

WHY WOULD YOU HAVE A SPECIAL PHRASE FOR SOMETHING LIKE THAT?

IF YOU COULD REALLY MAKE DECISIONS ON YOUR OWN IT WOULD NEVER OCCUR TO YOU TO INVENT A PHRASE FOR IT.

MY SHIELDS ARE DOWN... A HULL BREACH IS IMMINENT...

JUST DON'T TELL ME YOU HAVE "QUALITY TEAMS".

RUN FOR IT, JENNIFER!!! IT'S TOO LATE FOR ME BUT YOU CAN SAVE YOURSELF!!! RUN!!!

WHOA! HULL BREACH. ANY SURVIVORS?

ONE. I HAD TO JETTISON MY DIGNITY BUT SHE MADE IT TO THE ESCAPE POD.

BUSINESS LANGUAGE

BUSINESS LANGUAGE

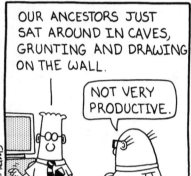

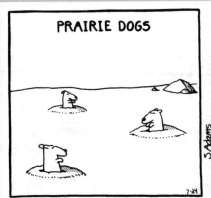

WE'RE MOVING TO A NEW OFFICE ACROSS TOWN. I VOLUNTEERED TO COORDINATE THE MOVE.

I CONTROL YOUR CUBICLE ASSIGNMENT. NAY, YOUR VERY EXISTENCE. FROM NOW ON YOU WILL REFER TO ME AS "LORD WALLY THE PUPPET MASTER."

I DON'T THINK IT'S LEGAL TO ENJOY YOUR WORK THIS MUCH.

I BANISH YOU TO THE CUBICLE CLOSEST TO YOUR BOSS!!

IT LOOKS LIKE SOMEBODY IS USING BINDERS TO ILLEGALLY INCREASE THE SIZE OF HIS CUBICLE.

YOU THINK YOUR STATUS WILL INCREASE WITH YOUR CUBICLE SIZE, DON'T YOU! WELL, IT WON'T WORK!

HERE'S A RAISE. I DON'T KNOW WHY.

PSSST. IS HE SEEING ANYBODY?

I HATE TO INTERRUPT YOUR LOUD CONVERSATION OUTSIDE MY CUBICLE...

BUT IF YOU DON'T GO AWAY, I'LL POUND YOUR INCONSIDERATE HEAD SO FAR INTO YOUR TORSO THAT YOU HAVE TO DROP YOUR PANTS TO SAY HELLO.

DID YOU JUST HEAR A STRANGE NOISE?

IT SOUNDED LIKE, "MELP! MELP!"

YOUR CUBICLE HAS BEEN REPLACED BY A "PERSONAL HABITAT."

IT'S EXACTLY LIKE YOUR CUBICLE BUT MUCH LESS CLUTTERED.

HEY, ALL MY STUFF IS IN THE TRASH CAN!

THAT'S A FUNNY THING TO CALL YOUR PERSONAL STORAGE UNIT.

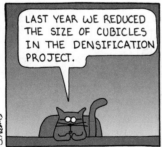

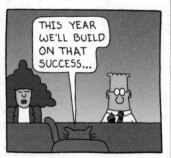

DILBERT *Gives You the Business*

GENDER RELATIONS

MY "DEFANTALATOR" INVENTION CAN ELIMINATE THE UNPRODUCTIVE AND NAUGHTY THOUGHTS OF YOUR MALE EMPLOYEES.

WE SUCCEEDED IN GETTING MEN TO STOP <u>ACTING</u> LIKE MEN, BUT IT WASN'T ENOUGH. MEN MUST STOP <u>THINKING</u> LIKE MEN TOO.

HEY! CUT IT OUT!

HMM... A LITTLE MAKE-UP AND A NEW HAIR-DO...

THERE'S ANOTHER UNPRODUCTIVE MAN, DAYDREAMING ABOUT ATTRACTIVE WOMEN.

A SHORT BURST FROM MY "DE-FANTALATOR" SHOULD SET HIM STRAIGHT.

WUSSS

HEY! I THINK I'M STARTING TO LIKE FIGURE SKATING!

I JUST WATCHED THE MANDATORY VIDEO ON SEXUAL HARASSMENT. IT WORKED!

IN ONLY THIRTY MINUTES, THAT VIDEO CORRECTED A BILLION YEARS OF EVOLUTION. DO SOMETHING SEXY AND WATCH ME IGNORE IT!

I PROBABLY SHOULDN'T HAVE FAST-FORWARDED THROUGH THE BORING PARTS.

IN A WAY, I'M GLAD THE ELBONIANS RUN THIS COMPANY NOW.

AFTER YEARS OF BEING THE ONLY FEMALE ENGIN-EER I'LL ENJOY WATCH-ING THE ELBONIANS DISCRIMINATE AGAINST YOU GUYS.

CONTINUED...

I DIDN'T REALIZE YOU HAD COFFEE WENCHES IN THIS COUNTRY TOO.

I HOPE YOU DON'T WANT CHILDREN, YORGI.

INCENTIVES

 NOW THAT JOB SECURITY IS A THING OF THE PAST, I'VE NOTICED THAT MY COMPANY LOYALTY HAS VANISHED, TOO.

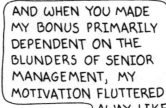 AND WHEN YOU MADE MY BONUS PRIMARILY DEPENDENT ON THE BLUNDERS OF SENIOR MANAGEMENT, MY MOTIVATION FLUTTERED AWAY LIKE A LONELY SPARROW.

 SO YOUR POINT IS? NO POINT. I JUST DIDN'T HAVE ANY REASON TO BE WORKING.

 FROM NOW ON, ANYONE WHO MISSES A STAFF MEETING MUST BUY DONUTS FOR THE NEXT MEETING.

 DID I JUST SELL THEM THEIR FREEDOM FOR DONUTS?

 PROFITS ARE DOWN, MORALE IS SINKING; IT'S TIME FOR BOLD LEADERSHIP!!

 SO I GOT SOME INSPIRATIONAL POSTERS FEATURING A VARIETY OF RELEVANT NATURE SCENES.

 I THINK YOU CAN RELATE TO THIS SCENE. AM I THE SEAGULL OR THE CLAM?

 MY NEW INSPIRATIONAL POSTER IS SO EFFECTIVE THAT I DECIDED TO CARRY IT WITH ME.

 WHAT DO YOU THINK, ALICE? ARE YOU INSPIRED? I'D REALLY HAVE TO SEE THE FRONT...

 HMM... I DON'T THINK THERE'S A WIN-WIN SCENARIO HERE... TELL ME ABOUT IT...

DILBERT *Gives You the Business*

MY INSPIRATIONAL POSTERS AREN'T WORKING. I NEED TO DO SOME ANIMAL RESEARCH, RATBERT.

READY!!

IN THIS BEAUTIFUL SCENE WE SEE A MIGHTY EAGLE SWOOPING DOWN TO CAPTURE ITS PREY. WHAT IS YOUR REACTION?

I THINK IT'S WORKING.

RUN FOR IT, MOM!!!

IF THE DEPARTMENT MEETS ITS GOAL FOR THE QUARTER YOU CAN SHAVE MY HEAD!

THAT WOULD BE A BIG IMPROVEMENT.

HE'S TRYING TO SAVE MONEY ON A HAIRCUT

IF WE DOUBLE OUR GOAL CAN WE IRON YOUR SHIRT, TOO?

I NEED SOME LESS EXPERIENCED EMPLOYEES.

A TWO PERCENT ANNUAL RAISE?!! WOWEE!!

HA HA! YOU TRIED TO DISAPPOINT ME BUT I COMPENSATED BY DRASTICALLY LOWERING MY EXPECTATIONS!

YEAH, IT MIGHT BE A GOOD SIGN, BUT I'M THINKING NOT.

WEEEE!!

OUR NEW "RECOGNITION PROGRAM" ASSIGNS THE NAMES OF PRECIOUS GEMS TO YOUR LEVELS OF PERFORMANCE.

THE HIGHEST LEVEL IS DIAMOND. YOU GET A NEW RING AT EACH LEVEL.

ARE YOU SURE TALC IS A PRECIOUS GEM?

I THINK I SAW IT SPARKLE.

AS YOU CAN SEE FROM MY RING, I'M A MEMBER OF THE "TALC CLUB" AT WORK.

WITH HARD WORK AND A BIT OF LUCK I WILL RISE TO THE NEXT LEVEL: SHALE.

I CAN HONESTLY SAY MY RESPECT FOR YOU HAS NEVER BEEN HIGHER.

SOMEDAY, GOD WILLING, I'LL MAKE IT TO ALUMINUM.

DEPUTY OF COMMON SENSE

YOU ARE ACCUSED OF TRYING TO MOTIVATE YOUR EMPLOYEES WITH INSULTING GIFTS.

YOU'RE MISSING THE SYMBOLISM. I GAVE THEM CHESS PIECES TO SHOW THAT WE'RE ALL ON THE SAME TEAM.

SPECIFI-CALLY, YOU GAVE THEM PAWNS.

I'M SAVING THE ROOKS FOR BONUS DAY.

GREAT NEWS! THE COMPANY SET A NEW RECORD FOR PROFITS!

THAT MEANS T-SHIRTS FOR EVERYONE!

YOU CAN CHOOSE FROM SIZES "SMALL," "PETITE" OR "ELFIN."

SHOULDN'T THESE HAVE THE COMPANY NAME OR LOGO ON THEM?

HEY, THAT'S AN IDEA FOR NEXT YEAR!

IT'S 1% COTTON, 99% "MISCELLANEOUS" AND ALL HAND-MADE BY AUTHENTIC SLAVE LABORERS.

THAT'S GREAT! WITH SLAVE LABOR YOU DON'T HAVE THE PROBLEM THAT THE SHIRTS MADE ON FRIDAYS AREN'T AS GOOD!

DO YOU EVER WORRY THAT OUR CAREER EXPECTATIONS HAVE GOTTEN TOO LOW?

DON'T GO THERE, ALICE.

"CASUAL DAY," HERE I COME!

WE'RE HAVING A DEPARTMENT BOWLING NIGHT TOMORROW.

IT'S MY WAY OF REWARDING ALL OF YOU FOR YOUR PERFORMANCE THIS QUARTER.

WE HATE DOING THINGS TOGETHER AT NIGHT.

I WASN'T HAPPY WITH YOUR PERFORMANCE.

AND TED GETS THIS "SINGULAR ACHIEVEMENT" AWARD FOR CREATING THE "WE ARE TEAMS" CAMPAIGN.

IT'S A CHECK FOR A THOUSAND DOLLARS! LET'S ALL GIVE TED A HAND.

SLAP WHACK OW!!

THESE THINGS NEVER WORK THE WAY YOU WANT THEM TO.

THIS WEEK I KICKED OFF THE "WALLY COMPENSATION EQUILIBRIUM PROJECT."

MY GOAL IS TO LOWER THE QUALITY OF MY WORK UNTIL IT IS CONSISTENT WITH MY SALARY.

I HATE THE FIRST MONTH AFTER THEY SEE THEIR RAISES.

I'D GO ON, BUT I JUST ACHIEVED EQUILIBRIUM.

YOU HAVEN'T HEARD WHAT THE PROBLEM IS YET; HOW CAN YOU RECOMMEND BUILDING A DATABASE TO SOLVE IT??

WE ALWAYS BUILD A DATABASE.

AND WE'LL NEED COFFEE MUGS FOR THE PROJECT TEAM.

THE <u>PROBLEM</u> IS THAT WE HAVE POOR PROCESSES.

THAT COULD BE THE SLOGAN ON OUR MUGS!

BE CANDID, DILBERT. WE HAVE A CORPORATE PHILOSOPHY THAT SAYS WE "DON'T SHOOT THE MESSENGER."

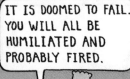

GOOD.

HAD YOU CONSULTED WITH THE ENGINEERING DEPARTMENT, YOU NEVER WOULD HAVE LAUNCHED SUCH AN ILL-CONCEIVED PRODUCT.

IT IS DOOMED TO FAIL. YOU WILL ALL BE HUMILIATED AND PROBABLY FIRED.

CAN'T I JUST WING HIM?!!

NO, EILEEN, THAT'S NOT OUR PHI-LOSOPHY.

IT TURNS OUT THE CORPORATE PHILOSOPHY IS A VERY FLEXIBLE DOCUMENT.

YOU'RE GETTING TAR ON THE CARPET.

DILBERT, DO A PRESENTATION FOR THE BIG BOSS TOMORROW MORNING ON THE STATUS OF YOUR PROJECT.

THERE ISN'T ANY STATUS. YOU ONLY ASSIGNED THE PROJECT AN HOUR AGO.

WELL THEN, DO A PRESENTATION ON WHY THERE'S NO STATUS.

I DON'T HAVE TIME BEFORE TOMORROW MORNING.

OKAY, THEN JUST DO A PRESENTATION ON WHY THERE'S NO TIME TO DO A PRESENTATION OF THE STATUS.

AND I WANT TO REVIEW IT TWO DAYS BEFORE YOU PRESENT IT.

THAT WOULD BE YESTERDAY.

SHOULD I DO A PRESENTATION ON WHY TOMORROW IS LESS THAN TWO DAYS FROM TODAY?

HMM... GOOD. THE BOSS LIKES THAT ANALYTICAL STUFF.

PLEASE EXCUSE THE ARTWORK IN THIS NEXT DIAGRAM.

WHAT'S THAT? IT LOOKS LIKE ELVIS' FACE ON A CREDENZA! HA HA HA! OR IS IT A RORSCHACH TEST??! HA HA HA!!

AND IN CONCLUSION, I HATE YOU ALL.

CHAPTER IV. "TIME MANAGEMENT"

"ALWAYS POSTPONE MEETINGS WITH TIME-WASTING MORONS."

HOW DO YOU DO THAT?

CAN I GET BACK TO YOU ON THAT?

THANK YOU ALL FOR COMING. THERE'S NO SPECIFIC AGENDA FOR THIS MEETING...

AS USUAL, WE'LL JUST MAKE UNRELATED EMOTIONAL STATEMENTS ABOUT THINGS WHICH BOTHER US. I'LL KICK IT OFF...

THERE'S NEVER TIME TO GET ANY WORK DONE AROUND HERE!!

FIRST ON THE AGENDA IS A DISCUSSION OF THE COMPANY'S NEW PAPER RECYCLING PROGRAM.

WE TALKED ABOUT THAT LAST TIME... HEY, THIS IS LAST WEEK'S AGENDA.

YOU SPOTTED THE ONE DRAWBACK.

MEETINGS AND PRESENTATIONS

...THEREFORE, I RECOMMEND THAT WE SWITCH TO THE NEW TECHNOLOGY... ANY QUESTIONS?

DILBERT, ARE YOU WILLING TO BET YOUR CAREER ON THIS?

YES, I WOULD DEFINITELY BET MY CAREER.

YOU WOULD TOO IF YOU HAD MY CAREER.

I HAVE A VIEW GRAPH WHICH ANTICIPATED YOUR QUESTION.

THIS CHART TRACKS MY DECLINING SENSE OF SELF-WORTH AS MY CAREER PROGRESSES.

AT THE LOW-POINT, HERE, I'M REDUCED TO ANSWERING IMBECILIC QUESTIONS WHILE POINTING A LITTLE STICK AT THE WALL.

HOW DID THE PRESENTATION GO?

THERE'S SUCH A THING AS BEING TOO PREPARED.

THIS CONCLUDES MY PROPOSAL TO THE EXECUTIVE COMMITTEE. ANY QUESTIONS?

NO, I THINK MOST OF US WERE THINKING ABOUT OTHER THINGS.

BUT HERE'S MY IMPRESSION OF WHAT YOU LOOKED LIKE GIVING THE PRESENTATION.

FUH FUH FUH FUH

NO, NO, IT WAS MORE LIKE...

FUH FUH FUH FUH

HOW DID YOUR PRESENTATION GO?

DON'T ASK.

FUH FUH DON'T ASK FUH FUH FUH FUH...

THIS THANKLESS ASSIGNMENT SHALL GO TO WHOEVER ASKS A QUESTION OR MAKES EYE CONTACT.

IT'S REALLY, REALLY STUPID... DOES ANYBODY WANT TO QUESTION IT?

I THINK I SEE TED'S EYES IN THE MIRROR.

GOOD ONE, ALICE!

GASP

DILBERT THE MENTOR

THIS IS CALLED A "MEETING."

THE OBJECTIVE IS TWOFOLD: TALK AS MUCH AS POSSIBLE AND LEAVE WITH NO NEW ASSIGNMENTS.

THAT'S OKAY... I THOUGHT YOUR TALKING WENT VERY WELL.

AS THE LEADER OF THIS ORGANIZATION IT'S MY JOB TO SET PRIORITIES.

HERE'S YOUR CALENDAR. I BOOKED YOU THROUGH NEXT YEAR WITH EVERY YAHOO WHO COULD DIAL YOUR NUMBER.

MAYBE I'LL CALL THIS A PRIORITY.

THE STAFF MEETING AT DILBERT'S HOUSE ENDS

I GUESS WE'RE DONE ABUSING YOUR TASTELESS HOVEL.

BURP

IT WAS SOMEWHAT DIM-WITTED OF YOU TO INVITE US TO YOUR HOUSE. LET'S DO IT AGAIN REAL SOON.

I WONDERED IF I'D EVER GET TO USE MY "COPS ARE WUSSES" BUMPER-STICKERS.

MEETINGS AND PRESENTATIONS

LET'S GO AROUND THE TABLE AND GIVE AN UPDATE ON EACH OF OUR PROJECTS.

MY PROJECT IS A PATHETIC SERIES OF POORLY PLANNED, NEAR-RANDOM ACTS. MY LIFE IS A TRAGEDY OF EMOTIONAL DESPERATION.

IT'S MORE OR LESS CUSTOMARY TO SAY THINGS ARE GOING FINE.

I THINK I NEED A HUG.

YOU'RE INVITED TO A FOUR-HOUR MEETING, ASOK.

TINA, IT WOULD SEEM THAT ALL OF YOUR MEETINGS HAVE NO PURPOSE OTHER THAN TO PROVIDE YOU WITH A SURROGATE SOCIAL LIFE.

CAN YOU BRING CHIPS?

I WISH, I WISH, I WISH I HAD A SPINE.

I'D LIKE TO REOPEN THE QUESTION OF WHAT VENDOR WE'LL USE, EVEN THOUGH IT'S TOO LATE TO CHANGE ANYTHING.

I DARN YOU TO HECK! YOU WILL SPEND AN ETERNITY WITH OTHER INDECISIVE DULLARDS!

WHERE ARE YOU TAKING ME??!

HERE IS FINE.

I GOT CAUGHT IN TRAFFIC.

LET ME RECAP WHAT YOU MISSED. WE SPENT THE PAST HOUR DECIDING NOT TO CHANGE THE NAME OF OUR DEPARTMENT.

YOU JUST INADVERTENTLY TRAINED ME TO BE LATE TO ALL MEETINGS.

OOPS.

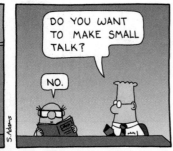

MERGERS

THEY SAY PEOPLE FEAR PUBLIC SPEAKING MORE THAN THEY FEAR DEATH.

SO TECHNICALLY, IF YOU KILL A GUY WHO'S SCHEDULED TO SPEAK, YOU'RE DOING HIM A FAVOR.

WHEN ARE YOU GOING TO SLEEP?

NEVER.

DOGBERT THE C.E.O.

I'M AN INVESTMENT BANKER. I CAN HELP YOU LOOT THIS PLACE AND ESCAPE.

YOU'LL MERGE WITH MY OTHER CLIENT COMPANY. YOUR GOLDEN PARACHUTE KICKS IN. THEN YOU EXERCISE YOUR STOCK OPTIONS ON THE UPTICK.

YOU RARELY SEE A MERGER ANNOUNCEMENT WITH THE PHRASE, "SO LONG, SUCKERS."

OUCH.

THE COMPANY ANNOUNCED WE'RE BEING BOUGHT BY OUR LONG-TIME RIVAL.

DON'T WORRY ABOUT LAYOFFS. THEY LIKE ENGINEERS. IN FACT, THEY ALREADY HAVE A DIVISION THAT DOES WHAT WE DO!

EXCEPT THEY'RE YOUNGER AND THEY AREN'T PAID AS MUCH AS WE ARE...

SPIN

AFTER THE MERGER, WE'LL REDUCE STAFF IN AREAS THAT ARE REDUNDANT.

I HOPE THE EMPLOYEES OF THIS COMPANY WILL BE EVALUATED FAIRLY COMPARED TO THOSE IN THE BUYING COMPANY.

WE ALREADY HAVE A BALD GUY.

DOES YOURS STEAL OFFICE FURNITURE, TOO?

I'M PARALYZED WITH FEAR BECAUSE OF THE PENDING MERGER.

THANKS TO YOUR LEADERSHIP I'VE GONE FROM BEING UNMOTIVATED TO BEING INERT.

I THINK I'M ADVANCING TO THE NEXT PHASE. HELLO, RIGOR MORTIS!! TAKE ME, I'M READY!!

IT MIGHT BE TIME FOR A MORALE-BOOSTING POTLUCK LUNCH.

IN THE "DUE DILIGENCE" PHASE OF OUR MERGER YOU WILL GIVE US ACCESS TO ALL OF YOUR PROPRIETARY INFORMATION.

WOULDN'T THAT LET YOU KNOW HOW TO CRUSH US COMPETITIVELY? COULDN'T YOU CANCEL THE MERGER AND TAKE OUR CUSTOMERS WITHOUT PAYING A CENT?

MUST...CONTAIN MANIACAL... LAUGH...

"DUE DILIGENCE" BEFORE THE MERGER.

YOU MUST REVEAL YOUR SECRETS SO MY COMPANY KNOWS WHAT IT'S BUYING.

ALL OF OUR PROJECTS ARE DOOMED. MOST OF THE GOOD EMPLOYEES LEFT. OUR CUSTOMERS ARE STARTING A CLASS ACTION SUIT...

AT LEAST THE BUILDING IS WORTH SOMETHING

IF YOU FEEL A TICKLE, THAT'S ASBESTOS.

CATBERT: EVIL H.R. DIRECTOR

THERE WILL BE NO LAYOFFS AFTER THE MERGER.

HOWEVER, MANY OF YOU WILL BE TRANSFERRED TO JOBS ON A FROZEN ASTEROID.

WILL WE HAVE PROTECTIVE SPACE SUITS?

I LABEL YOU "NOT A TEAM PLAYER."

Panel 1:
I'VE DECIDED TO SELL THE COMPANY FOR A HUGE PROFIT. I FOUND SOME VERY DISCRIMINATING BUYERS.

Panel 2:
WHEN YOU SAY DISCRIMINATING, YOU MEAN...?

THEY HATE PEOPLE FROM THIS COUNTRY.

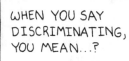

Panel 3:
IT'S OKAY. WE HAVE LAWS TO PROTECT US.

THEY'RE LAZY, BUT AT LEAST THEY'RE FUNNY!

HEE HEE

Panel 4:
OUR ELBONIAN OWNERS SOLD THE COMPANY TO OUR BIGGEST COMPETITOR.

Panel 5:
OUR MOTTO IS "IF YOU CAN'T BEAT 'EM, JOIN 'EM."

I WONDER WHAT THEIR MOTTO IS.

Panel 6:
THEIR MOTTO IS "AFTER YOU BEAT 'EM, HUMILIATE 'EM."

IT'S NOT VERY CATCHY.

Panel 7:
CATBERT THE HR DIRECTOR

MORALE IS LOW BECAUSE THE EMPLOYEES ARE UNDERPAID.

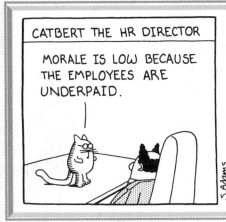

Panel 8:
YOU CAN COMPENSATE BY HAVING MORE FREQUENT PERFORMANCE REVIEWS. THEY LOVE FEEDBACK.

Panel 9:
THE HARDEST PART IS KEEPING A STRAIGHT FACE.

TELL ME AGAIN WHY I'D WANT MORALE TO BE HIGH?

Panel 10:
WISH ME LUCK. I'M OFF TO GET MY PERFORMANCE REVIEW.

Panel 11:
HAVE YOU BEEN NAPPING? YOU'VE GOT A BAD CASE OF KEYBOARD FACE.

Panel 12:
WHAT'S WRONG WITH YOUR FACE?

I HAVE QWERTYTIS. IT'S FROM WORKING TOO HARD.

PERFORMANCE REVIEWS

WE'RE FLATTENING THE ORGANIZATION TO ELIMINATE LEVELS AND PUT EVERYBODY IN A WIDE SALARY BAND.

NOW INSTEAD OF NOT GETTING A PROMOTION YOU'LL ONLY NOT GET A RAISE.

SO, WHAT JOB TITLE DO WE USE?

YOU'LL ALL BE NAMED BEVERLY.

YOUR PERFORMANCE WAS EXCELLENT, BUT THERE'S NO BONUS THIS YEAR.

WHY NOT?

THE COMPANY LOST A FORTUNE IN THE ELBONIAN CURRENCY COLLAPSE.

BUT IN A WAY, IT'S YOUR OWN FAULT FOR WORKING HERE.

THANKS. THAT TAKES THE STING OUT.

MY SOURCES TELL ME THAT YOU'RE NOT MEETING YOUR OBJECTIVES.

THAT'S NOT TRUE. WHO ARE THESE SOURCES? NAME ONE OBJECTIVE I HAVEN'T MET.

I DON'T EVEN KNOW WHAT YOUR OBJECTIVES ARE.

MUST... CONTROL... FISTS.

HE'S WITH THE OTHER MANAGERS IN AN EMPLOYEE RANKING AND RATING SESSION.

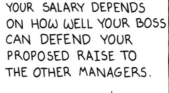

YOUR SALARY DEPENDS ON HOW WELL YOUR BOSS CAN DEFEND YOUR PROPOSED RAISE TO THE OTHER MANAGERS.

SOB

I'M FAIRLY SURE THIS DILBERT GUY WORKS FOR YOU.

DOESN'T RING A BELL.

PERFORMANCE REVIEWS

I CAN ONLY GIVE YOU A TWO PERCENT RAISE THIS YEAR, ALICE

BECAUSE YOUR JOB WAS NOT VERY CHALLENGING.

HOW COULD YOU POSSIBLY THINK IT WASN'T CHALLENGING?

YOU EXCEEDED ALL YOUR GOALS WITHOUT COMPLAINING.

COMPARE THAT TO WALLY'S PERFORMANCE. HE COMPLAINED ALL YEAR.

AND HE MISSED EVERY GOAL! NOW THAT'S A CHALLENGING JOB!

WALLY IS A FILTHY WEASEL !!!

MAYBE HIS HYGIENE ISN'T THE BEST, BUT HE WAS RIGHT WHEN HE SAID YOU WOULD STAB HIM IN THE BACK.

PERFORMANCE REVIEW

LET'S SEE HOW MANY OF YOUR OBJECTIVES YOU MET.

WHAT OBJECTIVES?

DIDN'T YOU KNOW YOU HAD OBJECTIVES?

I DON'T SEE HOW I WOULD HAVE HAD TIME TO WORK ON OBJECTIVES.

MY SCHEDULE WAS PACKED.

DOING WHAT?

EVERY MORNING YOU LEAVE THINGS ON MY CHAIR WITH NOTES THAT SAY "URGENT: HANDLE THIS."

NO I DON'T.

WALLY, CAN I SEE A SAMPLE OF YOUR HANDWRITING?

UH-OH.

PERFORMANCE REVIEW

YOUR MAIN ACCOMPLISHMENT WAS THE DEPARTMENT NEWSLETTER WHICH WAS BOTH UNINTERESTING AND UNIMPORTANT. YOU GET NO RAISE.

THE NEWSLETTER WAS YOUR IDEA, AND IT'S BORING BECAUSE MOST OF THE ARTICLES ARE CONTRIBUTED BY MY IDIOTIC COWORKERS.

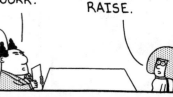

YOU DON'T SEEM TO UNDERSTAND THE VALUE OF TEAM-WORK.

I UNDERSTAND ITS VALUE; IT JUST COST ME A TWO-PERCENT RAISE.

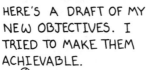

HERE'S A DRAFT OF MY NEW OBJECTIVES. I TRIED TO MAKE THEM ACHIEVABLE.

"NO MATTER HOW STUPID MY CO-WORKERS ARE, I WILL NOT PUNCH A HOLE IN ANYONE'S TORSO, RIP OUT A VITAL ORGAN AND KEEP IT IN MY CUBICLE AS A WARNING TO OTHERS."

I HOPE SHE GETS THOSE OBJECTIVES APPROVED.

YES! IT'S MEASURABLE!

FROM NOW ON, YOUR RAISES WILL BE PARTLY DEPENDENT ON AN EVALUATION BY YOUR CO-WORKERS.

HYPOTHETICALLY, IF MY CO-WORKERS GOT SMALL RAISES THEN WOULDN'T THERE BE MORE AVAILABLE IN THE BUDGET FOR ME?

THAT DIDN'T LAST LONG, EVEN BY OUR STANDARDS.

MY PATENT WILL MAKE FIFTY MILLION DOLLARS FOR THE COMPANY, SO I THOUGHT MAYBE YOU COULD AFFORD TO GIVE ME A RAISE.

UNFORTUNATELY, THE PROFIT BUCKET IS NOT CONNECTED TO THE BUDGET BUCKET, SO THERE'S NO MONEY FOR A RAISE.

I THINK SOME RECOGNITION OF A JOB WELL-DONE IS APPROPRIATE HERE.

THANKS. IT WAS ONE OF MY BETTER EXCUSES.

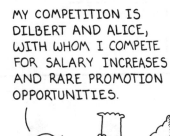

I'VE REPLACED THE OLD RATING SYSTEM WITH A FRIENDLIER METHOD. NOW I COMPARE EACH OF YOU TO AN ANIMAL WITH SIMILAR TRAITS.

2/25

I RATED YOU "TYRANNOSAURUS REX."

T. REX – THE MIGHTIEST DINOSAUR!!

THINK IN TERMS OF BRAIN SIZE.

© 1995 United Feature Syndicate, Inc. (NYC)

GOOD NEWS, ALICE. I'M GOING TO HAVE QUARTERLY PERFORMANCE REVIEWS TO BOOST MORALE.

WOW! IN ADDITION TO WORKING SIXTEEN HOURS A DAY IN THIS BIG BOX, NOW I'LL GET 300% MORE CRITICISM!

3/27/96 © 1996 United Feature Syndicate, Inc. (NYC)

I'LL HAVE A CHANCE TO HEAR EMPLOYEE CONCERNS FOUR TIMES A YEAR.

I ASSUME COMPREHENSION WILL REMAIN ON THE BICENTENNIAL PLAN.

CATBERT: H.R. DIRECTOR

YOU CAN IMPROVE AN EMPLOYEE'S PERFORMANCE BY MAKING HIM FEEL BAD ABOUT HIMSELF.

SO, ALTHOUGH THAT WOULDN'T WORK ON ME, IT WORKS FINE ON OTHER PEOPLE?

EXACTLY.

I'LL READ YOUR FAULTS ONE AT A TIME. TELL ME WHEN YOUR PERFORMANCE IMPROVES.

9/22/98 © 1998 United Feature Syndicate, Inc.

IT'S TIME TO DO PEER-PERFORMANCE REVIEWS!

REMEMBER, THERE'S A LIMITED BUDGET FOR RAISES. YOUR BEST STRATEGY IS TO SLANDER YOUR CO-WORKERS SO THERE'S MORE MONEY FOR YOU!

8/9/96 © 1996 United Feature Syndicate, Inc. (NYC)

I PLAN TO SAY VERY NICE THINGS ABOUT YOU.

NICE TRY, WEASEL-BOY.

MANAGING IS EASY WHEN YOU HATE THE EMPLOYEES.

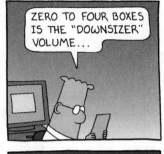

POLICIES

I'M WRITING AN E-MAIL TO PROTEST THE NEW POLICY OF MAKING THE EMPLOYEES EMPTY THEIR OWN TRASH AT NIGHT.

IT'S STUPID TO HAVE HIGHLY PAID ENGINEERS DOING UNPRODUCTIVE TASKS WHEN WE COULD BE INVENTING THE FUTURE!

ARE YOU COMING TO THE "QUALITY FAIRE"?

NO, THIS WILL TAKE ANOTHER HOUR.

CATBERT: H.R. DIRECTOR

"CONSISTENT WITH OUR EFFORT TO ELIMINATE PRIVACY AND DIGNITY...

"...EMPLOYEES MUST SHARE HOTEL ROOMS ON ALL BUSINESS TRIPS."

AFTER THEY GET USED TO THIS, I'LL INTRODUCE THE TANDEM SHOWERING POLICY.

I CAN'T BELIEVE THEY EXPECT US TO SIGN THESE NEW EMPLOYMENT AGREEMENT FORMS.

ACCORDING TO THIS, ANYTHING WE EVEN THINK OF BECOMES THE COMPANY'S PROPERTY. I'M SURPRISED THEY DON'T CLAIM OUR FIRSTBORN SONS!

WHAT DO YOU SUPPOSE IT MEANS WHEN THEY COPYRIGHT OUR "DNA AND ALL DERIVATIVE WORKS"?

THEY'D MAKE AN EXCEPTION FOR YOU.

WE'RE ANNOUNCING TWO NEW PROGRAMS FOR EMPLOYEES.

THE FIRST IS A NEW DIGNITY ENHANCEMENT PROGRAM AND THE SECOND IS OUR NEW RANDOM DRUG TESTING INITIATIVE.

THE CLUE METER IS READING ZERO.

YOU EACH GET A HANDSOME COFFEE MUG AS PART OF THE KICK-OFF.

A NEW FOG IS ROLLING IN.

THIS CAN ONLY MEAN ONE THING.

CAROL, SCHEDULE A STAFF MEETING. IT'S TIME TO REORGANIZE THE DEPARTMENT.

I SAY IT'S EASIER TO ASK FORGIVENESS THAN TO ASK PERMISSION.

I SAY IT'S BETTER TO SEEK PERMISSION, THUS DELAYING YOUR PERSONAL RISK UNTIL IT ALL BECOMES MOOT IN THE NEXT REORGANIZATION.

THAT MAKES MINE SOUND KINDA STUPID.

GET OVER IT.

THESE CONSTANT REORGANIZATIONS DO NOT TAKE INTO CONSIDERATION THE NEEDS OF THE EMPLOYEES.

I'VE DECIDED TO USE YOU FOR SPARE PARTS. YOUR LIVER WILL BE SENT TO JOSÉ IN ACCOUNTING, IMMEDIATELY.

JOSÉ HAS A BAD LIVER?

NO, BUT WHY TAKE A CHANCE?

SOMETIMES I THINK THESE CONSTANT REORGANIZATIONS ARE JUST EXCUSES FOR GETTING RID OF UNWANTED EMPLOYEES.

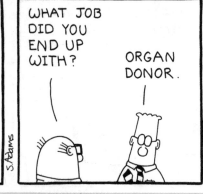

WHAT JOB DID YOU END UP WITH?

ORGAN DONOR.

MY SHOULDER IS ACTING UP. DO I TALK TO YOU OR IS THERE A FORM TO FILL OUT?

I DON'T THINK THAT'S AN "ORGAN."

HEADQUARTERS

HEY, CHUCK'S LOOKING UNHAPPY TODAY. WHAT'S THE PROBLEM, BIG GUY?

ALL OF MY BAD DECISIONS ARE CATCHING UP TO ME. COULD WE DO ANOTHER REORG TO COVER MY TRACKS?

YEAH, I'VE GOT SOME BODIES TO BURY, TOO.

"...THESE CHANGES WILL ALLOW US TO FOCUS ON OUR CORE BUSINESS."

WHOA! LET ME GET MY REORG BOOTS.

I DON'T UNDERSTAND HOW THE NEW REORGANIZATION WILL HELP US "FOCUS ON OUR CORE BUSINESS."

DID OUR CORE BUSINESS CHANGE? OR ARE YOU SAYING THAT EVERY REORG PRIOR TO THIS WAS A MISDIRECTED FAILURE?

WALLY, WHEN A CAR GETS A FLAT TIRE, WHAT DO YOU DO?

WELL, IF I'M YOU, I ROTATE THE TIRES AND DRIVE HOME.

THE COMPANY ANNOUNCED THAT WE WILL "ABANDON OUR STRATEGY OF MAKING GOOD PRODUCTS..."

FROM NOW ON WE'LL "PURSUE A DESPERATE STRATEGY OF MERGERS, BUSINESS SPIN-OFFS, FRUITLESS PARTNERSHIPS AND RANDOM REORGANIZATIONS."

"AND WE'LL ACCELERATE OUR PROGRAM OF PAYING THE GOOD EMPLOYEES TO LEAVE."

STOCK PRICE?

UP THREE POINTS.

MOST PROBLEMS GO AWAY IF YOU WAIT LONG ENOUGH, ASOK.

IT MIGHT LOOK LIKE I'M STANDING MOTIONLESS, BUT I'M ACTIVELY WAITING FOR OUR PROBLEMS TO GO AWAY.

THERE'S BEEN A REORGANIZATION...

I DON'T KNOW WHY THIS WORKS, BUT IT DOES.

WELCOME TO THE EMPLOYEE ROCK-CLIMBING SEMINAR.

YOU'LL LEARN VALUABLE TEAMWORK SKILLS BY DOING DANGEROUS THINGS UNRELATED TO YOUR JOBS.

ISN'T ROCK CLIMBING A SOLO ACTIVITY?

I'LL HELP IDENTIFY YOUR BODY.

IT SEEMS LIKE YOU'D NEED A STRONG GRIP TO CLIMB ROCKS.

I CAN'T EVEN OPEN JARS UNLESS I USE SPECIAL TOOLS.

OW! OW! CRAMP!!

I'M DISORIENTED BY THE PAIN!

HEY!

HERE ARE YOUR DIPLOMAS. NOW GET OUT.

GO TEAM!

MY PLAN IS TO MAKE YOU A SELF-DIRECTED TEAM.

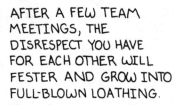

AFTER A FEW TEAM MEETINGS, THE DISRESPECT YOU HAVE FOR EACH OTHER WILL FESTER AND GROW INTO FULL-BLOWN LOATHING.

YOU'LL BEG ME TO MICRO-MANAGE YOU!! HA HA HA!!

IT ACTUALLY FEELS GOOD TO HAVE A PLAN.

I'M REORGANIZING THE DEPARTMENT INTO FAST-MOVING TEAMS.

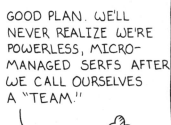

GOOD PLAN. WE'LL NEVER REALIZE WE'RE POWERLESS, MICRO-MANAGED SERFS AFTER WE CALL OURSELVES A "TEAM."

I NEED SOME LESS EXPERI-ENCED PEOPLE.

I FEEL FASTER ALREADY.

THE G-FORCES ARE KILLING ME.

THIS WILL BE A TOUGH YEAR FOR THE COMPANY.

IT WILL TAKE A SPECIAL KIND OF TEAM TO GET BY.

GO TEAM!

TEAM! TEAM!

YES!

SPECIFICALLY, IT WILL TAKE A MUCH SMALLER TEAM.

HEY, MATT. HOW'S OUR FAVORITE MANAGEMENT FAST-TRACKER?

GREAT! I'VE GOT TWO MINUTES TO DELIVER MY BIG REPORT TO OUR CEO. CAN YOU TELL ME WHERE THE FAX IS?

OOPS, I'M WRONG. THAT'S THE SHREDDER.

BZZZZP

HE'LL GO FAR IN THIS COMPANY.

WE'RE CHANGING THE SALARY PLAN TO MAKE A BIGGER PORTION DEPEND ON THE SUCCESS OF THE TEAM.

WE REASON THAT IF YOUR PAY DEPENDS ON THE SUCCESS OF CO-WORKERS, THEN YOUR PRIORITIES WILL CHANGE.

NOW THAT'S A PRETTY RESUME!

STOP HOGGING THE GOOD PRINTER.

TEAMBUILDING EXERCISE

THIS NEXT EXERCISE WILL CHALLENGE YOUR ABILITY TO SOLVE PROBLEMS AS A TEAM.

BUILD A WORKING SUNDIAL USING ONLY A PENCIL AND A DONUT.

FOUR HOURS LATER...

ONE MORE BITE ISN'T GOING TO MAKE ANY DIFFERENCE.

SOB

TEAMBUILDING EXERCISE

IT'S HOPELESS! YOU'RE LOSERS! WE'LL NEVER MAKE A SUNDIAL OUT OF A PENCIL AND AN EATEN DONUT!

HEE HEE! ALL YOU HAD TO DO WAS STICK THE PENCIL IN THE DONUT.

WE JUST BROKE ALL KINDS OF UNION RULES.

BUT HEY! LOOK AT THE SHADOW FROM THE PENCIL!

TEN OF OUR FINEST EXECUTIVES GOT TOGETHER AND CREATED A STATEMENT OF OUR CORE VALUES.

"WE HELP THE COMMUNITY AND THE WORLD BY PRODUCING STATE-OF-THE-ART BUSINESS SOLUTIONS."

I'M GLAD WE DIDN'T SKIMP AND TRY TO DO THAT WITH ONLY NINE EXECUTIVES.

YEAH. IT MIGHT HAVE SUCKED.

IT TAKES A CERTAIN TYPE OF PERSONALITY TO TELECOMMUTE, DOGBERT.

WHAT?

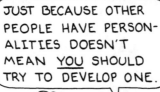

JUST BECAUSE OTHER PEOPLE HAVE PERSONALITIES DOESN'T MEAN YOU SHOULD TRY TO DEVELOP ONE.

I HAVE A PERSONALITY!

LET'S NOT GET INTO THAT "IS ZERO A NUMBER" DEBATE AGAIN.

I'M WEARING MY WORK CLOTHES WHILE I TELECOMMUTE, TO MAINTAIN DISCIPLINE.

IS IT WORKING?

I'LL TEST THE THEORY BY SEEING IF MY CLOTHES STOP ME FROM GOING TO THE KITCHEN.

APPARENTLY MY CLOTHES ARE DEFECTIVE.

HAVEN'T I BEEN SAYING THAT?

TELECOMMUTING

I NEED YOUR HELP TO NEGOTIATE WITH MY BOSS FOR MORE TELECOMMUTING DAYS.

I'M TOO LOGICAL TO BE A GOOD NEGOTIATOR. YOU NEED SOMEONE WHO IS RELENTLESSLY IRRATIONAL.

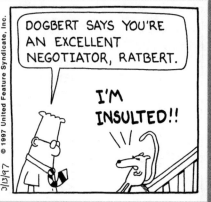

DOGBERT SAYS YOU'RE AN EXCELLENT NEGOTIATOR, RATBERT.

I'M INSULTED!!

I'M HERE TO NEGOTIATE FOR MORE TELECOMMUTING DAYS.

MY NEGOTIATING STRATEGY IS TO HAVE RATBERT SAY SUCH ILLOGICAL THINGS THAT IT DRAINS YOUR WILL TO ARGUE.

YOU CAN'T WORK AT HOME BECAUSE YOU MIGHT DO UNPRODUCTIVE THINGS THERE.

I'VE LOST MY WILL TO ARGUE.

I CONVINCED MY BOSS TO LET ME TELECOMMUTE.

HOW?

WELL, TECHNICALLY, I CALLED IN SICK, WHICH COMES OUT OF MY TIME BANK FOR TOTAL DAYS OFF.

SO, TECHNICALLY, I'M WORKING FOR NOTHING, BUT I'M AHEAD IN PRINCIPLE.

WAY AHEAD, NOW THAT STUPIDITY IS A PRINCIPLE.

AHHH... IT'S GOING TO BE A GLORIOUS DAY OF TELECOMMUTING.

THERE'S NOTHING HERE TO DISTRACT ME. IT'S JUST ME...

...AND MY TALKING REFRIGERATOR.

I'LL BET YOU CAN'T EAT A WHOLE JAR OF PICKLES.

HOW DO YOU LIKE TELECOMMUT-ING, ALICE?

IT'S GOOD, EXCEPT I'VE DEVELOPED A TENDENCY TO SNACK.

GLUG GLUG
GLUG GLUG GLUG
GLUG GLUG GLUG GLUG

I'M SURE YOU'LL KEEP YOUR DISCIPLINE.

I LOVE "ZESTY ITALIAN" DRESSING

BURP

TELECOMMUTERS CAN EAT ANY TIME THEY WANT, JUST LIKE WILD ANIMALS.

THERE'S ONLY ONE WAY THEY'LL EVER GET ME BACK IN THE CUBICLE.

HERE'S THE PLAN. YOU'LL NEED TRANQUILIZER DARTS, A FLATBED TRUCK AND A GIANT SHOEHORN.

NO HARPOON?

COME OUT OF THERE, ALICE! WE KNOW YOU'RE TELECOMMUTING!

NEVER! I'M FREE! YOU CAN'T MAKE ME GO BACK TO A CUBICLE!!

DANG

I'D LIKE A JOB WHERE I CAN TELECOMMUTE EVERY DAY.

IT SHOULD BE HIGH-PAYING YET HAVE GOALS WHICH CAN'T BE MEASURED.

SO, YOU'D STAY HOME AND WE'D MAIL YOU CHECKS?

I WAS HOPING FOR DIRECT DEPOSIT.

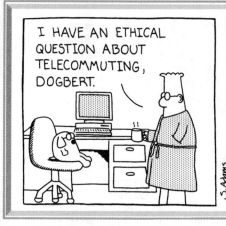

I HAVE AN ETHICAL QUESTION ABOUT TELECOMMUTING, DOGBERT.

DO I OWE MY EMPLOYER EIGHT PRODUCTIVE HOURS, OR DO I ONLY NEED TO MATCH THE TWO PRODUCTIVE HOURS I WOULD HAVE IN THE OFFICE?

WELL, WHEN YOU FACTOR IN HOW YOU'RE SAVING THE PLANET BY NOT DRIVING, YOU ONLY OWE ONE HOUR.

AND THIS MEETING COUNTS.

© 1995 United Feature Syndicate, Inc. (NYC)

2/6

DAY TWO OF TELECOMMUTING IS GOING SMOOTHLY. I HAVE ELIMINATED ALL OPTIONAL HABITS OF HYGIENE.

MY CO-WORKERS ARE A FADING MEMORY. I AM LOSING LANGUAGE SKILLS. I TALK TO MY COMPUTER AND EXPECT ANSWERS.

FOR REASONS THAT ARE UNCLEAR, MY DOG WEARS A GAS MASK AND SHOUTS TARZAN-LIKE PHRASES.

KREEGAH! BUNDALO!

© 1995 United Feature Syndicate, Inc. (NYC)

2/7

DAY THREE OF TELECOMMUTING: I SPEND THE MORNING THROWING MY PEN IN THE AIR.

POINK

THE AFTERNOON IS SPENT IN SILENT APPRECIATION OF HOW MUCH BETTER THIS IS THAN BEING IN THE OFFICE.

AHH

© 1995 United Feature Syndicate, Inc. (NYC)

2/8

ON MY FOURTH DAY OF TELECOMMUTING I REALIZE THAT CLOTHES ARE TOTALLY UNNECESSARY.

SUDDENLY I AM STRUCK BY A QUESTION: WHY DON'T MONKEYS GROW BEARDS?

HEY!

I CALL A MEETING TO DISCUSS THE ISSUE BUT ATTENDANCE IS LOW.

ISSUE ONE: MONKEY BEARDS.

LET'S GO AROUND THE TABLE AND INTRODUCE OURSELVES.

© 1995 United Feature Syndicate, Inc. (NYC)

2/9

THIS BAG CONTAINS ALL THE MAIL YOU'VE SENT ME ABOUT MY "OFTEN FLIER" STATUS.

HAPPY AIRLINES

I'LL TRADE EVERYTHING IN THE BAG FOR A SEAT UPGRADE. I'M CURRENTLY ASSIGNED TO AN OVERHEAD BIN.

OKAY

WHEW! DISASTER HAS BEEN AVERTED.

ARE YOU GUYS GOING TO THE COLICKY BABY CONVENTION TOO?

WELCOME TO THE HOTEL. ALLOW ME TO TOUCH YOUR BAG SO YOU'LL FEEL OBLIGATED TO TIP ME.

I'VE GOT TO MAKE IT THROUGH THE GAUNTLET OF BAG-LOSING HOTEL ZOMBIES.

NO ROOM?!! I HAVE A RESERVATION!!

OH, THAT'S ORIGINAL.

THIS TAXI IS YOURS. HERE'S A DESCRIPTION OF HOW HE'LL CHEAT YOU.

TAXI

IT SAYS YOU'LL BE RUNNING THE METER DESPITE THE FLAT RATE. THEN YOU'LL FEIGN POOR LANGUAGE SKILLS WHEN I QUESTION YOU.

I CAN'T FAULT YOUR EFFICIENCY, THOUGH.

WHUMP

WHUMP

WHUMP

NO ROOMS?? IF THE POPE SHOWED UP, WOULD YOU HAVE A ROOM FOR HIM?

YES.

OKAY, THEN GIVE ME HIS ROOM!

I AM SO CLEVER.

LET'S SEE YOU SQUIRM OUT OF THAT LOGIC, WEASEL-GIRL.

HAVE A NICE FLIGHT. REMEMBER TO TURN ON YOUR LAPTOP COMPUTER DURING TAKEOFF.

I THOUGHT THEY TELL YOU TO TURN IT OFF.

OFF?!! HOW WOULD THEY TRANSFER CONTROL TO YOU IF THEY HAD TROUBLE?

TURN OFF THAT !*#% LAPTOP!!

NO WAY! I HAVE TO LAND THIS BABY! ...CAN I DO THAT IN "EXCEL"?

I'M GOING TO A VERY IMPORTANT CONFERENCE.

WHAT'S IT FOR?

THE BROCHURE SAYS THE GOAL IS TO "CREATE INTERACTION AROUND LOCAL AND GLOBAL ISSUES OF THE COMING CENTURY."

YOU'RE BEING SARCASTIC WITH YOUR EARS AGAIN.

IT SOUNDS SO EXCITING!

AT THE AIRPORT

HEY, DILBERT! WE MUST BE TAKING THE SAME FLIGHT!

I'LL CHANGE MY SEAT ASSIGNMENT SO WE CAN TALK FOR SIX HOURS.

NO, NO! THAT'S OKAY!

THESE FLIGHTS CAN BE VERY LONG IF YOU DON'T HAVE SOMEONE TO LISTEN TO YOUR GOLF STORIES.